Be A More Effe

Battle blends positive thinking with "how-to" practicality, showing the reader ways to effectively plan, train, administer, manage and communicate.

Brux Austin
Former Editor-in-Chief, **Texas Business Magazine**

Battle's personal experience and success in volunteer leadership qualifies him well to offer these thoughtful guidelines. This handbook is a key resource for those who are challenged with more effective volunteer management.

Dan Bullock, Former Director
Texas Governor's Office of Community Leadership

A must for any officer in a volunteer organization. It gives you the tools to make your experience more rewarding.

David Hicks
Former Vice-President, Jaycees International

Battle hits the nail on the head with his paradoxical belief that it is impossible to contribute more to an organization, no matter how hard one tries, than one receives in return. Those willing to understand this secret will gain unlimited insight from this unique book.

Tim Richardson
Former Editor, **The Quorum Report**

This book is an insightful approach to managing, motivating and mobilizing volunteers. The principles are sound and have been developed from first-hand experience.

Kevin Krepinevich, 25th Executive Vice President
U. S. Junior Chamber of Commerce

This handbook is a must for any organization or individual seeking success in the volunteer arena.

Duane M. Leach, Ph.D.
Former President, University of Texas of the Permian Basin

THE VOLUNTEER HANDBOOK

THE VOLUNTEER HANDBOOK

HOW TO ORGANIZE AND MANAGE
A SUCCESSFUL ORGANIZATION

by
Richard V. Battle

BE A MORE EFFECTIVE VOLUNTEER !

Volunteer Concepts
P.O. Box 27584
Austin, Texas 78755
1-512-261-7015
volunteer@ibm.net

Library of Congress No. 88-50078
ISBN No. 0-929174-01-1

Third Printing May 1999

Manufactured in the United States of America
Armstrong Printing, Inc.
Austin, Texas

DEDICATION

To all who give selflessly of their time in order to help other people, this book is humbly dedicated.

FOREWORD

Volunteerism is a uniquely American custom and is a source of our country's enduring strength. Individuals freely give their time to educational, cultural, civic, welfare and religious causes. They provide services and opportunities which cannot be measured with a price tag. This has been an essential partner in America's growth and progress and would have a profoundly negative effect, if stopped. Individuals in our society are more productive, effective and fulfilled as they reinvest their time, energy and resources into their hometowns.

The best volunteer is a trained one; someone with the skills, knowledge and desire to efficiently interact with other volunteers. These skills are valuable tools, both in the volunteer and business sectors, and are vital to America's commerce and development.

Richard Battle's book is an effective "how to" guide for volunteers. It speaks to those who would like to become involved in organizations; to those already involved who are moving into positions of responsible leadership; and to those veteran officers who can use it as a reference and refresher.

Practical suggestions and plans of action are spelled out in a well-organized volume. It is written from Battle's extensive experience as a Jaycee and community volunteer. Partially a product of Jaycees training, Battle practices what he preaches with stunning success. He was selected outstanding Jaycees president of the world and his Austin, Texas chapter was also judged number one in the United States during his tenure. Jaycees is a leadership laboratory for young people to hone lifelong skills furthering the cause of volunteerism. Battle has also been a trainer for numerous Jaycees and other organizations.

Having worked closely with him for three years on a statewide project, I can attest to his formidable organizational abilities and knowledge of what works.

This book is a blueprint to successful leadership. Its lessons and suggestions are easily implemented and produce demonstrable achievements. No volunteer leader, chairman or officer should be without it.

John Ben Shepperd

Past U.S. Jaycees President

Past State of Texas Attorney General and
　　Secretary of State

December 1987

TABLE OF CONTENTS

INTRODUCTION

This book was written for individuals who want to improve their volunteer organizations. it offers ideas that will be helpful for the newest groups to the most sophisticated organizations. Individuals who want to organize a group will learn how to plan, organize and manage the group. Topics will include planning, training, administration, personnel management, finances, communications and public relations.

Although it is intended for volunteer groups, many of the ideas discussed can be utilized in business.

It is intended for use as a reference book of specific ideas that can be referred to by topic or read in total. I have tried to include as many specific ideas as possible. There are books available on several of the individual topics included, but my hope is that this volume can serve as a single volume that discusses the majority of topics of interest to volunteer groups. I use the term "activity" througout the book to mean a project, task, event office, or a responsibility. I also refer to an individual volunteer as "he" and not as "he/she" for the sake of simplicity.

It is also important to remember that there are no absolute answers. It is up to you to take this information and adapt it to your specific organization.

It is my belief that one of the greatest freedoms in a free society is that the people have the freedom to choose to volunteer for their choice of groups, their level of involvement and their time commitment. The need for volunteers is greater than ever in our society. Citizens should help their communities by volunteering their time to minimize governmental involvement.

Volunteer groups need to plan and run their organization like a business. Their most important duty is to perpetuate the organization by training future leaders. Properly training these leaders will also build a consistency of success that all organizations desire.

President Ronald Reagan in 1981 spoke on the importance of all people volunteering to help their fellow citizens. He stressed the value of those contributions to our society in money, time and strengthening our way of life. His appeal for volunteers:

"IF NOT YOU, WHO?

IF NOT NOW, WHEN?"

was simple, but pointed to the fact that we all are our brother's keeper.

Volunteer groups improve the quality of our lives. It is my deep desire that this book will help volunteers everywhere in their efforts to improve our society.

THE INDIVIDUAL VOLUNTEER

"Hope sees the invisible, feels the intangible and achieves the impossible."

Author Unknown

THE INDIVIDUAL VOLUNTEER

The Most Important Person

The most important person in an organization is the individual member. He contributes money, ideas and labor. By uniting with others in like causes, he is able to make a difference in the outcome of a given cause.

Millions of people volunteer every year in the United States alone. We often forget how important the contributions of a candy striper in a hospital, a boy scout troop leader, a fundraiser for a charity, a little league coach, committees for the arts, etc. truly are in our society. Without them, we would have a lower quality of life or higher taxes if the government tried to assume their functions.

Ways Volunteers Help an Organization

Quite often organization members become angry with fellow members who do not attend every meeting and activity. We must remember that people join an organization for different reasons. Also, any contribution to the organization is better than doing nothing. Sidney Smith said it best when he said: "It is the greatest of all mistakes to do nothing because you can only do a little. Do what you can." Too many of our citizens take their citizenship for granted. They do not volunteer for any group and are takers of society rather than givers.

There are four ways individuals can contribute to a volunteer organization. They are:

- *Participate in Activities*

  This is the most common and the contribution that even the newest member recognizes. Getting members involved in activities is important so that you can have a successful activity, activate the member in the organization and train future leaders in the organization. Unfortunately, not everyone wants to participate in an activity. Some members may not like the individual activity, not have the talent necessary to contribute or may be long standing members who are burned out on that activity.

- *Money*

  Members pay dues, which contribute to the success of the organization. They also can contribute additional money or raise funds to finance the activities of the organization.

- *In Kind Donations*

  Often a business or individual wants to help but they cannot donate money or time. Donations of goods and services like office space, use of a copier or office furniture, soft drinks, supplies, etc., allow the individual or business another method to assist the organization. Planning the types of goods and services you need and recruiting members who may offer them to you will help you maximize your effectiveness.

- *Recruit New Members*

  New members are the lifeblood of a volunteer group. A continuous supply of new members is imperative to insure the future of the organization. A satisfied and enthusiastic member of your organization is the best person to recruit his friend, co-workers and even strangers to join your efforts. New members are excellent to recruit new members because they may know a different group of people and they don't realize that someone may say no.

- *Ideas*

  An area that is often overlooked as a way to contribute to the organization is contributing new ideas. Some members will not sell hot dogs at a carnival, solicit funds, donate money or recruit new members, but they are creative. These people can be an invaluable source of ideas. Their ideas can be implemented by the organization with other members providing the management, funds and manpower.

  Long standing members who have done every job in an organization are excellent sources of ideas and that may be all that they want to do now. Their ideas are old ideas, but because they have not been used in sometime, they are like new ideas to the current leaders and are just as good.

  Do Not ignore people who want to contribute ideas!

Why Volunteers Should Be The Best That They Can Be

As we have discussed previously, volunteers are an important part of any free society. They have the opportunity, yes opportunity, to make a difference by their actions.

A successful volunteer and volunteer organization should do their best because they will:

- *Help Their Community*
  Their actions will make a difference in the quality of life in their community. They must realize that they are providing services that would not be available if they were not performing them.

- *Help Their Organization*
  Their efforts will make a difference in their organization as we have discussed in the previous section.

- *Help Themselves*
  We do not mean financially, but in personal development. Their interaction with other people, training and experiences will make them a better citizen. Their experiences will motivate them to contribute more through other organizations and or other public services.

- *Be Recognized and Rewarded*
  People love to hear the words "thank you" and "you did a good job." By hearing those words and or receiving a certificate, plaque or trophy will increase their self confidence in themselves. Recognition of success also motivates people to contribute more to the organization.

People You Want To Attract and Beware of in Your Organization

In every organization, there are some people that become successful and some that do not. It is important for you to recognize the positive and negative signs that will tip you off about their character. Discerning between people that will be helpful to the organization and those that will not is a learned ability. These criteria will be helpful, but will not replace learning by the experience of dealing with people.

People You Want to Attract

Everyone wants to attract the best people to work with them. Traits that indicate a person will be successful include:

- *Persistence*
  These people are the ones who look for reasons to make their goals happen. They do not take no for an answer. They will find a way to overcome all obstacles in the way of accomplishing their goals.

The following quote sums it up best: "Nothing in this world can take the place of persistence. Talent will not; nothing is more common than unsuccessful men with talent. Genius will not; unrewarded genius is almost a proverb. Education will not; the world is full of educated derelicts. Persistence and determination alone are omnipotent. The slogan PRESS ON has solved and always will solve the problems of the human race."

—Calvin Coolidge

- *Selflessness*
  The number one priority for these people is helping the organization, their fellow members and their community.
- *Enthusiasm*
  Enthusiasm is contagious. You can attract others to assist you in achieving your goals if you are enthusiastic.
- *Goal Oriented*
  They have direction in their life and they will appreciate and understand the organization's goal setting process.
- *Dedication*
  They are not afraid of working long hard hours if they will achieve their goal.
- *Time Managers*
  Don't be afraid to recruit busy people. They respect your time, are organized and know how to manage their time.
- *Attitude*
  A positive attitude will help them to expect success. They also need to be open minded to receive training and constructive criticism, which will help them to achieve their goals.
- *Professional Expertise*
  Organizations need expertise in accounting, marketing, finances and other areas. Recruiting experts in your areas of need will improve your organization's impact.

If you recruit people who have all or most of these traits you will increase the odds that you will be successful.

Beware of These People

Unfortunately, most of us have worked with people who have been detrimental to our organization. They also have common traits, which in hindsight are as the cliche says, "plain as the nose on your face." Being aware of these traits and evaluating everyone you work with will minimize the negative impact these people will have on your group.

Beware of people with the following traits:

- *Excuses*
  People who always have an excuse for not accomplishing their goals are usually looking for those excuses.

- *Drum Beater*
  These people are always beating their own drum for all the glory and credit for an activity. They are usually so busy beating the drum that someone else is doing the work. If an activity is successful, there is always enough credit for everyone.

- *Braggart*
  They will tell you how great of a job they are going to do before it is time to begin an activity. They are usually the last to arrive, the first to leave and do less than anyone else involved in the activity.

- *Non-Achiever*
  If a person is not making his short term goals and does not respond to your management, they will probably not achieve the overall goal of the activity. Recognize this trait as early as possible so you can replace this person before it is too late to salvage a successful activity.

- *Talker*
  They are the most vocal person at a meeting, but usually do the least amount of work. They feel, that if they say enough at the meeting, people will think that they are doing a good job and are more powerful than they really are.

- *Fun Seeker*
  They only want to do the fun or easy jobs. If a job is difficult or out of the limelight, they will not do well at it.

- *Complainer*
  They are negative about everything. Like the proverbial rotten apple they will ruin the entire barrel (organization) unless you stop them. Do not allow them to continue or you will have major problems. Talk with them about their attitude, but if you can not convince them to change it, look for a non-offensive way to ask them to become less involved.

- *Award Seeker*
  They are always looking for the award before the activity is completed. The dictionary is the only place in the world where success comes before work.

- *Time Traveler*
  They operate on their own time schedule and expect you to operate on it also. They do not use a calendar and when you call to remind them about an appointment that you have with them, they will decide whether or not to see you based on the prevailing winds at the moment. They will not respect your time.

- *Fair Weather Committer*
  They will always commit to do everything, but rarely follow through when it becomes time to act. An example is, a person who says that they will attend a dinner and then they do not. They do not understand that the organization had to guarantee their meal and lost money because they would not say "no" earlier. Another example is, the person who commits to work at an activity and then does not show up. As manpower sub-chairman this destroys your plans, but this person does not understand what the word commitment means.

- *Finger Pointer*
  At the first sign of a problem, they disavow any responsibility and look for the closest person to point the finger of blame. They will never admit that they made a mistake and you will never hear them say "I'm sorry," but you will hear them say quickly, "It's not my fault."

- *Resume Builder*
  These people join an organization only to add credits to their personal resume. While they may belong to several groups, they are interested only in belonging and not in making a positive difference in the impact the group makes in the community.

Responsibility of an Elected or Appointed Officer

When members are elected or appointed to an office, they are no longer a volunteer! They have accepted and possibly taken an oath to be responsible for an activity or activities with the organization.

They should set an example for the members of the organization by their conduct.

They have an obligation to execute their responsibilities and insure the future of the organization. They must take the long term benefit of the organization into consideration on every decision that they are involved.

They should attend all activities in their area of responsibility, and as many other activities and meetings as possible.

They will have to recruit, delegate, train, motivate, manage, assist and reward people to help them accomplish their goals.

The final responsibility of their term is to motivate and train at least one, but hopefully more than one person to take their job for the next term.

The President

The president, or leader of the organization has the ultimate responsibility for its success. As President Harry Truman said, "The Buck Stops Here." He is responsible for all the activities and people associated with the organization.

In addition to having the positive traits we previously discussed in this section, the president must exhibit the following traits:

- *Farsighted*
  The president's decisions must be based on the long term benefit of the organization. Mentoring and training the future leadership will insure that the organization will survive.

  He should always be thinking ahead of his board and membership. This will minimize unanticipated problems and the personal and organizational stress that comes with adversity.

  Changes will occur in the community or constituents you serve. If you anticipate and recognize these changes, you will be able to adapt and change your organization's programs and activities to address the revised needs. If you try to solve new problems with old methods, you will eventually cease to impact your community and the organization will fail.

- *Creative*

  The president should respect the history and tradition of the organization. This does not mean you should fall into the trap of "It has always been done that way." New and alternate ideas should be sought out and considered. They will not always be utilized, but by thinking through the planning process on an activity everytime, you will uncover new ideas or wrinkles that can improve the activity.

  Think like your constituents. What activities will give the maximum benefit for the energies expended. Do not expend energies on activities that will not offer something to your constituents that they don't need, don't want or is provided by someone else.

- *Decisive*

  You will make mistakes during your term. You can minimize mistakes by better planning and management.

  Make your decisions to act, not to react. Do not make decisions not to fail, but to succeed.

  Decisiveness is imperative because an indecisive leader will accomplish little and not be able to motivate his people to action. Nothing can happen in our lives without a decision; consequently, no decision is in itself a decision. We do not get out of bed without a decision, drive to work, etc. Avoiding a decision will not make it vanish. It will only waste time and opportunities until you make the decision and move on to the next activity.

- *Motivator*

  The president sets the example for the organization. Their conduct will positively or negatively impact the image of the organization in the community and with your membership. Leading by example, means that you will pull your members to accomplish the goals of the organization instead of pushing them. You should be willing to do any job that you will delegate and your members should know this fact. A leader that asks others to do things that they would not do themselves will lose their members respect very quickly.

Be enthusiastic and always positive! Your members should never see or hear negativism from you. Negativism is a de-motivator. If you must say something negative, select someone whom you can confide in with your concerns. Your enthusiasm will attract people to help you in your efforts.

Remember, others will not be as dedicated to achieving the goals of the organization as you are. You must constantly communicate to the members the impact on the community of their efforts. Share your belief that their actions will make a difference in the community, and your beliefs will become their beliefs.

If possible, attend all of the functions conducted by the organization. Your attendance will show support of the activity and motivate the members participating. Become involved in the activity, but remember the prestige of the office that you hold. You are the president, and the image portrayed of a president taking tickets, or setting up tables is not as positive to the community as if you have a large number of volunteers doing this work and you are able to motivate the workers and represent the organization to the public.

One of the most important tasks is to motivate members to become the future leaders of the organization. They often do not have the ambition or confidence to seek leadership, but do have the capability. Positive input from you can positively change their lives. The confidence you instill in them can turn them from followers into leaders. One of the most gratifying things that a leader can have happen is for someone to come up to them and thank them for the words of inspiration that they gave them in the past that changed their life.

Conclusion

Your term as president will always be remembered as "Bill or Mary's year"—not 1987. The success or failure of your term will be discussed as "Bill or Mary's year was great" or "Bill or Mary's year was terrible." You, by your efforts and leadership, will decide how you will be remembered and how much impact your organization has on the community, your members and your own personal development.

PLANNING

"A winner is someone who sets his goals, commits himself to those goals, and then pursues his goals with all the ability given him."

Author Unknown

WHY PLAN?

Businesses, organizations and individuals all have the same needs and receive the same benefits from planning and goal setting.

While business planning is no surprise, few volunteer organizations or individuals are as serious about planning. Organizations spend more time planning the next activity than they do the future of the organization. Individuals spend more time planning a vacation than planning their personal lives.

Planning is not only important for success, but essential. The benefits of strategic planning are:

- It improves the image of the organization to the community and with its members by its appearance as a well managed organization.

- It makes the organization aware of its strengths so they can be used to overcome the organization's weaknesses.

- It makes the organization recognize its weaknesses so they can plan to compensate for greater success.

- It gives the organization a sense of past victories, which provides a strength and confidence that goals can be achieved.

- Written goals enable you to see possibilities, put a plan into action and execute it. Written plans make you think through the entire planning, execution, review, revision, and evaluation process. This thought process helps you to plan contingencies to overcome anticipated and unanticipated problems. It also permits you to measure progress during the year, which prevents arriving at the end of the year with a a surprise discovery that you did not make your goals.

- Written plans provide you a track to run on.

- Planning makes you set priorities and establish direction of the organization. Direction and prioritization equal a more efficient use of your volunteer's efforts. This means that you will provide maximum service to your community and have less volunteers leave because they feel that they are wasting their time.

- Planning forces you to be specific. Goals that are not specific are worthless. Include numbers and time deadlines.

- Planning defines reality. No group can do everything that they desire. Planning exhibits this, and dictates that you spend your quality time working toward achievable goals.

- Charges the organization to be responsible for its own success.
- Serves as a measure to sharpen decision making. Decisions should be made considering long term goals. Do not make decisions while only reflecting on the short term crisis.
- A good planning process will prevent you from rushing into an activity that can turn into a disaster.

Remember the 7 P's of planning for success!

Proper Prior Planning Prevents Pitifully Poor Performances!

I have seen the following humorous story about poor planning in several places, but do not know who wrote it. I hope that it confirms the previous discussion as to why good planning is important in every endeavor.

"I am writing in response to your request for additional information. In Block 3 of the accident report form, I put, quote, POOR PLANNING, unquote, as the cause of my accident. You said I should explain in more detail and I trust the following will be sufficient.

I am a bricklayer by trade. On the day of the accident, I was working alone of the roof of a new six story building. When I completed my work, I discovered that I had about 500 pounds of brick left over. Rather than carry the bricks down by hand, I decided to lower them in a barrel by using a pulley which was attached to the side of the building.

Securing the rope at ground level, I went up to the roof, swung the barrel out, and loaded the brick into it. Then I went back to the ground and untied the rope, holding it tightly to insure a slow descent of the 500 pounds of bricks. You will note in Block 11 that I weigh 135 pounds.

Due to my surprise at being jerked off the ground so suddenly, I lost my presence of mind and forgot to let go of the rope. Needless to say I proceeded at a rather rapid rate up the side of the building.

In the vicinity of the third floor, I met the barrel coming down. This explains the fractured skull and broken collarbone.

slowed only slightly. I continued my rapid ascent, not stopping until the fingers of my right hand were two knuckles deep into the pulley.

Fortunately, by this time I regained my presence of mind and was able to hold tightly to the rope in spite of my pain.

At approximately the same time, however, the barrel of bricks hit the ground, and the bottom fell out of the barrel. Devoid of the weight of the bricks, the barrel now weighed approximately 50 pounds.

I refer you again to my weight in Block 11. As you might imagine, I met the barrel coming up. This accounts for the two fractured ankles and the lacerations on my legs and lower body.

The encounter with the barrel slowed me enough to lessen my injuries when I fell onto the pile of bricks and, fortunately, only three vertebras were cracked.

I am sorry to report, however, that as I lay there on the bricks, in pain, unable to stand, and watching the empty barrel six stories above me, I again lost my presence of mind.

I let go of the rope."

LONG RANGE PLANNING

A written long range plan is essential to the long term success of an organization. It provides long term direction and stability to an organization. It also minimizes the opportunity of any one year's deviation from the plan causing negative long term effects.

The procedure to establish a Long Range Plan is:

- Establish a committee including past presidents, the current president, other current officers and additional important members.
- Study the history of the organization and previous long range plans.
- Use the historical information to project future needs of the organization.
- Solicit input from your membership.
- Develop ideas for improving the organization.
- Establish long range goals and action plans.
- Update the plan on an annual basis.

Topics to include in your Long Range Plan are:

 I. ORGANIZATION
  A. MEMBERSHIP—A significant growth in membership will necessitate several organizational changes.
  B. LEADERSHIP—Board structure, size, term of office, qualifications, etc.
  C. CONSTITUTION AND BY-LAWS
  D. PUBLIC RELATIONS
  E. PERSONNEL—Paid staff
 II. FACILITIES
  A. PROPERTY
  B. OFFICE
  C. EQUIPMENT
 III. FINANCE
  A. INVESTMENTS
  B. TAX EXEMPT STATUS
  C. 501C3 CHARITABLE ORGANIZATION STATUS— Many organizations are applying for charitable organization status so they can solicit tax deductible contributions. (This will be discussed further in the organization finances area.)
  D. FISCAL YEAR AND ACCOUNTING
 IV. PROGRAM OF WORK
  A. ALL LARGE ACTIVITIES

Every leader should care about the long term success of their organization. Long range planning provides the tool to maximize the probability that the organization will grow in a desired positive manner.

ANNUAL PLANNING

The steps in developing an annual plan,* which will follow in detail in the following pages, are:

Conduct the following pre-planning surveys.

- Organization Membership
- Community
- Incoming Board Members

Evaluate the surveys and list.

- Strengths and Weaknesses
- Community Needs
- Member Needs

Prioritize your lists.

- Management Weaknesses to Overcome
- Community Needs
- Member Needs

Set goals by priorities.

Establish activities to achieve goals.

Plan the Annual Calendar.

- Activities
- Public Relations
- Gantt Chart

Plan the Annual Budget.

- Annual Budget by Activity and Area
- Monthly Cash Flow Analysis
- Activity Budgets

Scheduled—Monitor, Evaluate and Revisions of Annual Plan

- Quarterly, Semi-Annual

Annual Evaluation of Program

* (Adapted from the United States Jaycees chapter planning guide.)

STEP 2—PRIOR TO YOUR ANNUAL PLANNING RETREAT
SURVEYS

Surveying your membership, community(served) and incoming board of directors is important in planning your programs and training. Each area will be discussed in detail, but first we will discuss general rules for conducting a successful survey:

- It should be no more than one page to prevent discouraging responses.

- Every question must be well thought out as to its purpose and wording to solicit unbiased responses.

- It should be simple to encourage responses. Questions asking the respondent to select one of a limited number of specific choices will be answered more frequently than questions with open ended answers.

- Utilize more than one method to solicit responses. Among the more common methods of surveying are mail, telephone, in person, brainstorming meeting and ads in the newspaper.

- Attempt to obtain enough responses to statistically validate your results.

- Seek assistance from a professional marketing researcher to insure proper wording of questions and to determine the number of responses necessary to validate the results.

- Publish the results for your membership and community showing them your sincere interest in their opinion.

- Most important, act on the results! If you do not plan based on outside input, people will think that you don't care and they will be less likely to respond to future calls for assistance.

MEMBERSHIP SURVEYS

If you don't offer the meetings, programs and activities that your membership is interested in, at the time they can participate, you will have a very difficult time obtaining member interest and participation in your programs.

Conduct the membership survey annually as a part of the annual planning process. All new members should be given a survey to find out their interests and get them involved in an activity as soon as possible.

Go out of your way to obtain survey responses from members who are not participating regularly. Their input may be invaluable in reactivating them in the organization.

Examples of questions that solicit membership information are:

1. Length of time in the organization: 0-6 months _____ 6-12 months _____ 1—3 years _____ 3 years _____

2. Marital Status: Single _____ Married _____ Name _____

3. Level of interest and involvement: High _____ Moderate _____ Low _____ None _____

4. What is the best day to hold membership meetings? M _____ T _____ W _____ Th _____ F _____ Sat_____

5. What is the best time to hold meetings? 7:00 a.m. _____ 12:00 noon _____ 6:30 p.m. _____

6. List your three most favorite activities conducted by the organization? A. _____ B. _____ C. _____

7. List three activities you like least: A. _____ B. _____ C. _____

8. Have you been contacted to work on an activity within the last six months? Yes _____No _____

9. How were you recruited into the organization? Personal contact _____Activity _____Advertising _____Social Event _____Self Initiative _____Other _____

10. Are you satisfied with our meeting location? Yes _____No _____If not, why? _____

11. What are your preferences for food entrees? Buffet _____Sandwich bar _____Pizza _____Steak _____Italian _____Chinese

_____Mexican _____Other _____

12. Are you satisfied with the overall quality of our speakers at meetings? Excellent _____Very good _____Good _____Average _____Room for improvement _____Suggested speakers or ideas: _____

13. Comments:

COMMUNITY SURVEYS

The purpose of surveying your community is to determine the public image of your organization, and to determine community needs for you to consider addressing during the year.

Surveying your local community and the constituency you serve provides an organization several benefits. They include:

- Responses will identify and rank needs of the community.

- Respondents of the survey will become more aware of your organization.

- Respondents are good sources for assistance on activities where they indicated that a need that you're asking for assistance with was a high priority. This assistance includes money, in kind (goods and services) donations, volunteer help and calling their friends for additional assistance. Only approach respondents after you have completed your plan and included their ideas. Showing them your plan will impress them with your organization and make them more likely to accept your request for help.

- Surveying community leaders and VIP's will also provide you an opportunity to solicit meeting speakers. Elected officials, business leaders, etc. are excellent people to approach for both needs of your organization.

- A question regarding membership will offer respondents an opportunity to request membership information. This should be a very soft sell.

Questions on a community survey may include:

1. Name—(optional)

2. Age—Select from a choice of age ranges.

3. Are you a member of a volunteer organization? Yes _____No _____

4. Are you familiar with **Your group's name**? Yes _____No _____

5. Are you aware of the following activities? Please indicate if you are aware that they are sponsored by **Your group's name**.

Example

			Know **Your Group's**
Activity	*Familiar With*		**Name** *Sponsors*
MDA Walkathon	Yes	No		Yes	No
American Cancer	Yes	No		Yes	No
10K Run	Yes	No		Yes	No

6. Which area of the community do you feel is the most important problem?

Example

_____Elderly Services   _____Drug Abuse

_____Education   _____Crime

_____Child Abuse   _____Underprivileged

7. We would appreciate your comments that would help our organization's efforts to improve our community.

_____

_____

8. Would you be interested in information on membership in Your group's name? Yes _____No _____

Mailing Address:

_____

People who are the best target group for your survey include:

- Elected Officials—Try to do these in person.
- Newspaper Editors
- Radio Station Managers
- Television Station Managers
- Corporate Leaders
- Religious Leaders
- Other Civic Groups
- Business Professionals—Doctors, Lawyers, etc.
- Members of Your Organization—This will also help you recruit committee members and a chairman for the activity that results from their input.

Once you have designed your survey, several techniques can be used to distribute the surveys. No one method is best in all circumstances and you may decide to use more than one technique.

These techniques include:

- Mail the survey to each individual. A cover letter introducing your organization and asking for his help is very important.
- Publish an ad in the newspaper and request the response be mailed to you.
- Conduct a telephone survey.
- Meet in person with selected community leaders.
- Door-to-Door canvassing of the community or a selected cross section of the community.
- Set up a booth at a high traffic location. A shopping mall is one example.

A successful community survey requires a significant amount of planning and hard work to conduct, but will provide your organization multiple benefits.

INCOMING BOARD MEMBER SURVEY

WHY

- It helps to place them in the proper board position based on their talent and interests.
- It exposes the member's talents.
- It exposes the member's weaknesses so that a training program can be planned for the group and individually to strengthen the board.
- It provides knowledge of future goals of the board members in the organization (i.e. President), so they can be trained, motivated and given the best opportunity to realize his goal.

QUESTIONS TO ASK INCOMING BOARD MEMBERS

- Length of membership.
- Previous offices and/or chairmanships they have held.
- Committees they have served on in the organization.
- Member's involvement in other organizations. This exposes potential overcommitment of the board member.
- Have you traveled to out of town organization meetings?
- Number of members you have recruited into the organization.
- What personal development training courses have you taken?
- What offices in the organization would you like to hold in the future?
- Can you attend all the meetings of the organization and the board of directors?
- Can you give money to the organization?
- Can you raise money for the organization?
- What committees are you interested in serving on?
- Why are you interested in serving on the board of directors?

This is an invaluable tool for the organization leader if it is used properly. It allows you to maximize the benefits for the organization and develop the future leadership in the organization.

AT YOUR ANNUAL PLANNING RETREAT

STEP 2—LIST: COMMUNITY NEEDS, MEMBERSHIP NEEDS AND STRENGTHS AND WEAKNESSES OF THE ORGANIZATION

Once you have compiled the results of your surveys, distribute the results to your board so it can use the information prior to and at the annual planning retreat. You are now ready to conduct your board planning retreat. The retreat begins with general topics and questions and moves toward specific goals and programs.

The first question at the retreat is to list the needs of the community, your membership and outline the strengths and weaknesses of the organization.

All needs should be listed with the prior understanding that no group can address every need or weakness in a given year. Also, some areas can not be addressed by a group in any year. An example might be that your community is in need of major road construction. Most groups can not attempt an activity of this type, but they can educate the community about the need or lobby for it with governmental authorities.

Divide strengths and weaknesses into areas by organization structure. An example of a strength might be that "the organization's treasurer is a CPA or banker." An example of a weakness might be that "the organization's treasurer has no experience in bookkeeping or handling finances." Normally, a strength will not also be listed as a weakness.

Maintain good records on how you obtained your information and identified the needs, strengths and weaknesses. This will be extremely beneficial when you begin your next needs identification process.

STEP 3—PRIORITIZE: COMMUNITY NEEDS, MEMBER-SHIP NEEDS AND ORGANIZATION WEAKNES-SES TO OVERCOME

After a complete list of needs, strengths and weaknesses has been compiled, they must be prioritized.

This should not be done by one person or a small group, but should involve the entire board of directors.

The number of issues you prioritize is subjective, based on the interests and resources of your organization. Four factors to consider when prioritizing the issues are:

- What is the financial requirement of the activity?
- What are the personnel requirements of the activity?
- Is there another group that is already working on this need, and would you be duplicating their efforts?
- What is the most serious or urgent problem?

STEP 4—SET GOALS BY PRIORITIES

Setting goals is the area where the planning process most often fails. Committing to a broad based general objective is easier than setting specific measurable goals.

For goals to be effective they must:

- **BE SPECIFIC, MEASURABLE AND INCLUDE A TIME DEADLINE.**
  An example is: To raise $5,000 for the Muscular Dystrophy Association by 12/30/87.
- **ASSIGN RESPONSIBILITY FOR ACHIEVING THE GOAL.** Assign one board member the responsibility for achieving the goal at the time it is included in the annual plan.
- **THE GOAL SHOULD BE REALISTICALLY ACHIEV-ABLE, BUT NOT EASY.**
  It is amazing the goals that people can achieve when they don't know that they can't do something and push themselves to the limit.

At the planning retreat, allow board members to set their own goals.

Often they will set goals higher than the President's and if it's their goal they will be more committed to achieving it. If the board member sets a goal that is too easy, then motivate him to raise the goal at the planning retreat or at one of the scheduled retreats during the year when the annual plan is evaluated and revised.

It is advisable to split up the board into groups by area of the organization for planning goals, activities, the calendar and budget for their areas. After each group has completed its planning, reassemble the entire group for discussion and approval of all plans.

STEP 5—ESTABLISH ACTIVITIES TO ACHIEVE THE GOALS

Once goals are established, activities to achieve the goals need to be planned.

The goals of the activities should follow the same rules as discussed in Step 4.

The sum of the goals of the activities in an area of the organization should be equal to the goals listed in Step 4.

Example -

Step 4 Goal—To raise $ 5,000 for the Muscular Dystrophy Association by 12/30/87.

Step 5

Activity 1— Raise $ 3,000 by conducting a golf tournament with 50 participants by 4/30/87.

Activity 2— Raise $ 2,000 by conducting a Walkathon with 100 participants by 9/30/87.

Activity 3— Raise $ 1,000 by conducting a bowlathon with 50 participants by 12/30/87.

Prioritize activities in each area by importance. If you discover during the year that you can not meet your goal and conduct all of your activities, put your major efforts toward your number one priority, number one goal and number one activity first. Prioritize additional efforts in descending sequence to assure the achievement of your top priorities.

STEP 6—PLAN ANNUAL CALENDAR

After priorities, goals and activities are planned and approved it is time to establish the annual calendar. Planning the calendar blends the plans of different areas of the organization into an overall organization plan.

The steps listed below will provide you a well planned calendar:

- Place large copies of each month's calendar of the year on the wall around your meeting room. Have all holidays, fixed date events and as many possible competitive events listed as possible. An example of an event that would be hard to compete against is trying to conduct an event in Dallas at the same time that the Dallas Cowboys are playing a football game. You will not realize the participation in the activity that you will by having it at another time.

- Have the secretary list all meetings, board meetings and state or national organization meetings.

- Have the officers from the various planning areas of the organization list their activities independently.

- In a session with the entire board, balance the calendar by moving activities from the months with more activities to the months with fewer activities planned. Take into consideration the time of the year (i.e. summer for vacations and winter for bad weather).

- After the calendar has been balanced, have the board of directors vote to approve it.

- The public relations director is responsible for working with the officers to plan the annual public relations plan and its calendar. (This will be discussed in more detail in the public relations section.)

- Train the board on the benefit of using individual calendars and how to list the organization's activities in their own calendar.

- Establish one person control for changes in the calendar. This is usually the secretary's responsibility. All changes must be cleared through this person. If you do not follow this rule, you will have 2 people making changes independently and the result will be 2 activities competing against each other for participants, manpower and publicity on the same day.

- Use board meetings and quarterly or semi-annual board planning sessions to revise the calendar as needed.

Following these steps will make your organization run more smoothly and maximize your personnel's efforts.

STEP 6a—GANTT CHARTS*

A Gantt chart is a calendar management tool that overcomes three problems most volunteer organizations experience:

- Because of a busy schedule, the planning process of most activities is not begun soon enough. This puts the activity behind immediately and inhibits its ability to reach its goals.

- Often activities are not managed for incremental progress, which results in the surprise awakening on the activity date that everything is not prepared properly.

- Most volunteers believe their responsibility ends on the activity date. This creates a problem after the activity with accomplishing tasks to wrap up the activity and submitting a final report to the board of directors.

Gantt charts are used in planning business operations from manufacturing to the construction industry. A simplified version is very helpful in volunteer activity management.

To utilize the Gantt chart:

- Design a form listing all activities, the area of the organization, the supervising officer and a calendar. (See example)

- List the activities on the form by organization area.

- Place a "C" in the week of the year signifying the activity date.

- Place a "D" 30 days after the "C" (activity) signifying the submission of a final report to the board of directors.

---

* Gantt Chart—In production planning and control, a type of base chart depicting the work planned and done in relation to time; each division of space represents both a time interval and the amount of work to be done during that interval. McGraw-Hill, *Dictionary of Scientific and Technical Terms,* Second Edition—1978, Edited by Daniel Lapedes.

Next come the two (2) most critical steps:

- Based on the size and complexity of the activity, decide the amount of time required to properly plan the activity. Once the required time is decided, subtract that time from the activity date "C" and place an "A" signifying recruitment of the activity chairman in the appropriate week.

- From the date that a chairman is recruited, calculate the length of time required to prepare a written plan for the board of directors. Add that time from the date a chairman is recruited "A" and place a "B" in the appropriate week to signify submitting the written plan for board approval.

- Add any other critical dates to the chart.

Once the chart is completed, the president, officer, board member or anyone else can determine if the activity is on schedule. Each week the schedule can be read to determine if any activity has a critical date due. If a critical date is due, the officer knows to follow up with the chairman to determine if the activity is on track.

If the activity is on track, everything is fine. If the activity is behind, the supervising officer will know it and be able to act immediately to get the activity back on track. This saving of precious planning time will significantly improve the results with all of your activities.

See the personnel management section regarding board members for additional information on how Gantt charts help you better manage your board of directors.

In review, Gantt charts are beneficial because:

- It alerts you to start activity planning on time.

- It enables you to manage activity progress on a regular basis to insure activity success.

- It defines a responsiblity and a due date to wrap up activity details and submit a final report to the board of directors.

AREA:

PAGE NO.:

SUPERVISING OFFICER:

MONTH	Jan.	Feb.	Mar.	Apr.	May	June	July	Aug.	Sept.	Oct.	Nov.	Dec.
WEEKS	0	4	8	12	16	20	24	28	32	36	40	44	48	52

EVENTS

LEGEND: A = Recruit Chairman, B = Submit Plan to Board, C = Project Date, D = Submit Finished Report

AREA: SUPERVISING OFFICER: PAGE NO.:

EVENTS	Jan.	Feb.	Mar.	Apr.	May	June	July	Aug.	Sept.	Oct.	Nov.	Dec.
WEEKS	4	8	12	16	20	24	28	32	36	40	44	48 / 52
AMERICAN HEART "WALKATHON"	A	B			C	D						
MUSCULAR DYSTROPHY GOLF TOURN.		A	B						C	D		

LEGEND: A = Recruit Chairman, B = Submit Plan to Board, C = Project Date, D = Submit Finished Report

STEP 7—PLAN THE ANNUAL BUDGET

Every organization should plan an annual budget. The treasurer of the organization is responsible for managing the overall budget.

After priorities, goals, activities and the calendar are established, it is time to plan the annual budget. The following suggestions will make your budget more functional.

- Divide the organization by areas for ease of management by board members.
- Have line items for all activities planned for the year.
- Have line items for all administrative expenses.

An annual budget is a tremendous tool, but sometimes timing of income and expenses becomes a problem. A **monthly cash flow analysis** is the tool that will help you forecast monthly income and expenses. This will permit you to schedule fundraisers if needed to offset planned expenses.

Budgeting and cash flow analysis will be discussed in much greater detail in the organization finances section.

The cash flow analysis is the final planning tool in establishing your annual plan. Now you're ready to lead your organization!

STEP 8—SCHEDULED MONITORING, EVALUATION AND REVISION OF ANNUAL PLAN

An annual plan is only useful if it is used as a **daily** management tool. The steps previously discussed give you organized techniques to simplify annual plan management. In addition to each board member managing his area daily, two types of evaluation sessions will make your plan more effective:

Quarterly or Semi-Annual—This is based on your organization size and amount of activity. A quarterly session will allow you to recognize deficiencies quicker so you can plan to correct your activity to achieve your goals. Similar to the annual planning retreat, you should have the meeting where you can not be disturbed. A Saturday is preferable because the session may take several hours.

The objective of this meeting is to:

- **Monitor your progress** by listing year to date results by goal and activity.

- **Evaluate results based on goals,** current conditions of the original need and other factors that will affect your interest in solving the need.

- **Revise your plan** as necessary. You may change priorities if a one becomes more important than another. You may raise or lower goals and you may add, delete, change or re-schedule activities.

Regular Board Meetings—A full scale review session normally can not be conducted at a board meeting, but four of the tools previously discussed should be reviewed at each board meeting:

- **Gantt Chart**—Review each board member's chart for completion of all tasks scheduled to date. For tasks that that have not been completed, have the responsible officer commit to a date for its completion.

- **Calendar**—Verify all upcoming activities and discuss and make all appropriate calendar changes.

- **Budget**—The treasurer is responsible to give a budget report at each meeting.

- **Cash Flow Analysis**—The treasurer is also responsible for reporting on variations from the cash flow analysis.

STEP 9—CONDUCT AN ANNUAL EVALUATION OF THE PLAN

At the end of the year, schedule a board meeting to conduct an annual evaluation of the organization's plan.

The evaluation should be written like the plan itself. Results of each goal and activity need to be listed. Finalize a year end budget at the same meeting.

The annual evaluation provides your organization the following benefits:

- It tells you what happened during the past year.

- It provides data necessary for producing an annual report for the organization.

- It will give next year's board of directors another source of input for planning the next year's goals and activities.

- It will document the organization's activities for historical purposes.

PLANNING RETREATS

A tool which can enhance the planning process is the planning retreat.

Annual Planning Retreat

This is the first opportunity for the new board to work together. It is important to provide a good working atmosphere, void of distractions, to conduct your planning process. A weekend out of town provides the best atmosphere. This also allows you to socialize together on Saturday evening, which also aids the team building process. Preparing for the retreat is critical as the new board members first board experience will occur on the retreat. A poorly planned or conducted meeting will make the new board member wonder whether or not they made a wise decision to join the board.

Quarterly Or Semi-Annual Retreats

These meetings are used to review, evaluate and revise your annual plan of action. They often can be conducted on a Saturday or in an evening. These events should be regularly scheduled from the beginning of the year, but the frequency is dependent on the organization.

HOW TO START A YEAR FAST

As the newly elected organization president, you face a real problem. How do I make sure that my year will start well without sacrificing the current year? You can have both, but it means that you must work overtime during the last month of the current year and the first month of the new year.

The following suggestions will insure your fast start:

- Do everything you can to insure the success of your organization this year. Your efforts in this area will have more impact than you can imagine for your entire year.

- Encourage your new board members to help their predecessors with their year end finish as a training tool.

- Begin the community and membership survey projects to identify the direction the organization will go next year.

- Survey your board members, which will help you plan the amount and type of training that they will need to start the year.

- Send incoming board members a welcome to the board letter. Include an important dates calendar so they know what is expected of them early and they can put these upcoming events on their calendar.

- Plan your weekend board planning retreat. A weekend out of town provides seclusion and a time to build comradarie that often is lost.

- Plan your annual awards banquet. This should be the most exciting event of the year in your organization. Everyone should be recognized, which will increase their interest for the coming year.

- **INSIST** that all board members attend your convention and officer training meetings. They will learn, obtain a broader perspective of the organization and have FUN!

- Plan transition projects during the last and first month of the year that will bridge the two years of the organization and maintain enthusiasm. Picnics or other social activities are good functions that are fun, a family activity and provide a forum for recruiting new members.

- Begin immediately preparing a list of prospective board members. Regardless of how wonderful your board is, turnover is inevitable. It is just a matter of time and quantity. The better prepared you are, the less negative effect turnover will have on your year.

You are standing on the threshold of opportunity. You have 365 days to positively influence your place in organization history. Your fast start will help your success.

HOW TO FINISH A YEAR STRONG

The last month of an organization's year is the most important. It is the month when successful people and organizations rise to the occasion and accomplish all of their goals. It is the most critical time for managing people and your organization plan. It is also a month to help your successor prepare for a fast start.

The President and President-Elect are the two most important people to insure a strong finish. Their responsibilities include:

President

- Total commitment that you will do **everything** possible between now and year end to make your year a success.
- Complete all activities! Work to improve their quality and impact.
- Conduct work sessions every Saturday and schedule week nights with your committees. This leading by example will motivate your team to excel.
- Encourage your members to run for the Board of Directors for the upcoming year. These individuals are trained and will also be helpful in closing the year strong.
- Promote teamwork! Every member needs to be reminded that any contribution that they make will help the organization (team) in your quest to be the best.
- Help the President-Elect plan the transition. Next year is your legacy. Your efforts will be more than repaid by people trying to help you finish this year strong.
- As Winston Churchill said, "Never Quit, Never Quit, Never Never Never Quit."

President-Elect

- A strong finish is the **No. 1** prerequisite to a fast start. Your efforts to selflessly insure a strong finish will be rewarded. Year end awards will motivate your board and membership.
- Motivate your new board members to help with the year end push. Encourage your new officers to work with their predecessors on their year end reports as a training tool.

The six greatest words of accomplishment that you can say to reflect on a successful year are, "I CAN, I WILL, I DID." Will you be able to look back on the year with these words?

ACTIVITY PLANNING

Conducting successful activities requires detailed planning similar to planning an organization's long range and annual plan.

Include the following items when an activity is planned:

- Assign one person the ultimate responsibility for the success or failure of the activity. Co-chairmanships sound nice, but the administrative and political problems encountered with this technique often are larger than the benefits received.

- The chairman needs to be creative. Do not plan it one way "because it has always been done this way." Think like the "buying public." If you are trying to raise money for a charity, sell the benefits of that charity to a targeted group you feel are more likely to respond positively to your request.

- The package you offer the public must be saleable. If you're planning a charity golf tournament, you may put together a great sponsorship package, but charge so high a price that no packages are sold. Knowledge of economic conditions and what interests the community, and what price you can receive for your package is critical.

- A good public relations plan will advise the market of what you are doing so they can participate, and expand your market by informing people who are not familiar with your organization or activity.

- Establish proper sales distribution channels. Whether you are selling raffle tickets, golf sponsorships, participation in an activity, etc., you must have an efficient method to sell or recruit the public to participate.

- Solicit input from the activity committee and public when planning the activity. This helps the committee "buy" into the activity because it becomes theirs. Input from individuals who showed interest on their survey form can provide you ideas, money, in kind contributions, manpower, etc.

- Establish a large committee for managing the activity. This will spread the workload to minimize overloading any committee member. It will also insure a large minimum participation in the activity as all committee members will participate in "their" activity.

- Put your plan in writing. Like the annual plan this is imperative. It offers the same benefits as previously stated in the "Why Plan" and "Annual Planning" sections.

Include the following steps in your activity plan *:

1. **What is the purpose of the activity?**
   Example—Conduct a goal setting for the community.

2. **List the specific goals of the activity.**

   These goals should be specific in quantity and have a time deadline.

   Example
   1—Conduct a goal setting seminar with 200 participants by 4/13/87.
   2—Obtain: 10 radio PSA's, 3 television PSA's and 2 newspaper announcements.

3. **List the activity committee and define their responsibilities.**

   Example of offices
   President
   Officer
   Chairman
   Sub-chairmen

   Example of how to list
   Manpower sub-chairman

   John Smith
   1234 Main St.
   Anytown, USA 12345
   (w) 123-555-1234
   (h) 123-555-4321

   John is responsible for recruiting, training and supervising all personnel for the activity.

4. List all materials and supplies necessary for the activity, the person responsible for their acquisition and the date when they are needed.

---

* Adapted from The U. S. Jaycees Chairman's Planning Guide.

Example

Date Due	Item	Person Responsible
1/ 2/87	Name Tags	Joe Jones
1/ 5/87	Soft Drinks	Mary Smith

List chronologically to assist in managing the sub-chairmen.

5. **List all non-organization people and organizations.**
   (Use this list as a telephone and mailing list. It is also helpful when you write your thank you letters.)
   Example

   1—Speaker
   Tom Smith
   123 Any St.
   Anytown, USA 98765
   (123) 456-7890

   2—Hotel
   Dew Drop Inn
   123 Highway 456
   Anytown, USA 98766
   (123) 457-5555
   Contact: Sally Jones

6. **List all "anticipated" problems and how you plan to overcome them.**

   (This is the tool for anticipating every possible problem and planning contingencies if the problem actually occurs. This step will minimize stress. If done properly, you will minimize the number of unanticipated problems. An unanticipated problem causes a crisis, and a crisis stresses the activity committee and retards its success.)

   Example

   Problem—The speaker will not show up for his seminar.

   Solution—Reconfirm the speaker the week and the day before the activity. Also, recruit a back-up speaker who can be prepared to participate if necessary.

7. **List the steps necessary to complete the activity.**
   (This is your chronological diary of all critical steps and who is responsible for their completion. At any date the chairman can look at this list and everything listed to that date should be completed. If a step is incomplete, the chairman can help the

sub-chairman complete the step and get the activity back on its schedule to a successful completion.)

Example

Date	Step	Person Responsible
1/ 5/87	Recruit Seminar Speaker	Joe Jones
1/10/87	Reserve Hotel Room	Mary Baker

8. **Complete the budget for the activity.**
   (Net results of the activity budget should comply with the annual budget.)

Example

Income	Proposed	Actual
Organization appropriation	$ 100.00	
200 participants @ $ 5.00	$1,000.00	
(List to include all sources)	_____	_____
TOTAL	$1,100.00	

Expenses

Hotel Room	$ 100.00	
Refreshments	$ 80.00	
Printing and Copying	$ 50.00	
Speaker's Gift	$ 20.00	

(List **every** expense item. Try to obtain donations for all items. This will be discussed further in the finance section.)

Return to Organization	$ 850.00	
(This is the net number that should match the annual budget.)	_____	_____
TOTAL	$1,100.00	

Once the plan has been written it should not be forgotten, but should be used as a daily management tool.

Referring to the activity plan daily offers the following benefits:

- It forces you to think about the goals you established and the daily tasks you planned to achieve those goals. This prevents you from falling too far behind on your plan.

- It keeps the pre-planned contingency alternatives fresh on your mind so they can be implemented with minimal delay and anxiety.

- It assists you in conducting a daily evaluation and writing of the progress of the activity, which will help the next time that you conduct the same activity.

The time from the date an activity is planned until it is completed and a final report is issued is the lifetime of the activity. An accurate record of the activity's life will help in planning and conducting that activity in the future. The activity's record will detail implementation of the plan and an evaluation of its results.

The following information will provide a complete record for the activity.

9. **Maintain a daily diary of the progress of the activity.**
   (The diary details the life of the activity. It is the completion of the steps planned in question number seven (7) of the planning process.

   Example

Date	Reference
1/1/87	Selected manpower sub-chairman.
1/5/87	Reserved room at hotel for seminar.
1/6/87	Submitted Public Service Announcement (PSA) to radio stations.
"	"
"	"
"	"
4/15/87	Conducted seminar.
"	"
5/12/87	Submitted final report to the board of directors.

10. **List the unanticipated problems and the changes you made to overcome them.**

    (This question details problems you did not plan for in question number 6 of the plan. It lists changes in the activity plan that were enacted to make the activity successful. It is very important for the future chairman of this activity to have this information so he will not make the same mistakes that you made.)

    Example

    Date   **Reference**

    1/10/87   Manpower sub-chairman was transferred out of town by his employer.

            We recruited a new sub-chairman the next day and proceeded with our plan.

    1/20/87   The hotel workers went on strike, which prevented our use of the hotel.

            We secured another hotel meeting room and will increase our public service announcements to inform the public of our change.

11. **List non-organization people and organizations who assisted in the activity.**

    (This list will help the next chairman of this activity know who donated time, money, goods or services so they can be asked to help the next time this activity is conducted. It also lists everyone who should be sent a "thank you" letter for his assistance. The "thank you" letter is important because it thanks the donor, tells how his contribution aided the overall success of the activity, and prepares him to be asked to assist the next time this activity is conducted.)

    Example

    Speaker   Tom Smith
    123 Any St.
    Anytown, USA 98765
    (123) 456-7890

Refreshments   Acme Cola Co.
                                                      555 First St.
                                                Anywhere, USA 87878
                                                     (123) 555-6666

12. **List activity income and expenses in chronological order. Also, complete the actual portion of the activity budget from question number 8.**

    (This question assists you in managing the budget and optimizing cash flow.)

    Example

Date	Reference	Income	Expenses
1/10/87	Appropriation from or- ganization	$ 100.00	
1/20/87	Printing—Ace Printing		$ 15.75
1/25/87	5—Tickets Sold @ $ 5	$ 25.00	

    (Continued)

	TOTAL	$ 125.00	$ 15.75

13. **List the results of the activity compared to your goals.**
    (This is the true test of the success of the activity. It is important to be as specific with your results as you were with your goals in question number 2 of the plan.)

    Example

    Goal 1— Conduct a goal setting seminar with 200 by 4/13/87.

    Results— We conducted the activity on 4/15/87 with 234 participants. This exceeded our goal of participants by 34.

14. **What changes would you recommend for conducting this activity in the future.**

    Example

    1. That the price for the seminar be raised next year to cover higher than anticipated costs.
    2. That a radio station be solicited as a co-sponsor to increase the potential for media exposure.

I recommend updating questions 9—14 daily, which will provide a more detailed and accurate final board report than possible if it is written after the activity. A simple way to maintain this record is by putting a blank sheet for each question in a 3 ring binder. Each day spend 15 minutes logging the day's progress onto the pages. By including your activity plan and all other activity documentation into the notebook, you will have a complete record of the activity plan, implementation and evaluation to pass along to the next chairman of the activity.

Summary

An activity plan like I have previously discussed is not easy the first time it is attempted. An attitude that the time spent on pre-planning will aid in the success of the activity currently and in the future is essential in making the planning process successful. The leadership of the organization must display this positive attitude in order to convince the membership that proper pre-planning is necessary.

Once the organization experiences the benefits of pre-planning, it will be accepted and encouraged by the membership. It is easier to conduct an activity when the chairman has a written record of the activity from the last time it was conducted, than it would be if the chairman had to conduct the activity from scratch.

ACTIVITY CHECKLIST

In spite of excellent planning, it is still possible to omit an item essential to the success of your activity.

Creating an activity checklist for your organization offers you an opportunity to insure that every detail is completed for your activities.

Once a checklist form is designed, it can be utilized for all of your activities. After the activity plan is approved, items on the checklist will be marked as they are accomplished.

Examples of items to include on your checklist are:

- Location
  - fee, if any
  - if it is outdoors, list an indoor back-up
  - parking
- Facilities at the site
  - size of the room
  - microphone
  - lectern
  - lights
  - sound equipment
  - directional signs
  - tables and chairs
  - flags and banners
  - kitchen, if applicable
  - restrooms

- Pre-activity paperwork
  - city approval
  - fire inspection
  - insurance coverage
  - contracts for use of location and other vendors

- Tickets
  - information to printer
  - distribution system (including advance sales)
  - number (for accounting purposes)

- Money
  - change box
  - change
  - table and appropriate signs
  - Method to collect advance sales
  - ticket sellers

- Manpower (plan your list and insert here)

- Administrative aids
  - receipts
  - pens and pencils
  - markers
  - material for signs
  - name tags

- Decorations
  - plates and cups
  - utensils
  - napkins
  - tablecloth
  - centerpiece
  - miscellaneous

- Food
  - bulk food
  - cooking and serving equipment
  - prepared meal—confirm menu and number of servings

- Publicity
  - press releases
  - invite the media representatives
  - press kits

- Finance
  - deposit receipts
  - charge card forms

- pay bills
- complete accounting

● Clean Up
  - assign manpower
  - donate leftovers to charity

● Miscellaneous

● Thank you's
  - to EVERYONE
  - Publicize individuals and businesses in your publication

● Post-activity paperwork
  - photographs of activity
  - complete written activity plan to benefit next chairman

List the person responsible for each task on the form and you have created a "to do" list for following up with all committee members.

TRAINING

"Today's preparation determines tomorrow's achievement."

Author Unknown

TRAINING

A problem in many volunteer organizations is that they do not spend enough time training their volunteers. They may not want to invest the time to train their people because they do not believe that it will lead to additional productivity. Another reason is that the people who are responsible for conducting the training are not properly educated on training their people.

Improper or insufficient training will lead to turnover of your people and less successful results than you may expect. Proper training will not only insure that the future of the organization exists, but that it will be more successful. A lot of organizations are successful for a year or two, but the mark of an excellent organization is that it is successful year in and year out. A commitment to training people from the top to the bottom in the organization will lead to a more consistent quality of leadership, which will produce more success for your organization.

The bottom line is that the time you invest in training your people will be far less than the success your organization achieves.

Before we discuss specific areas where training is necessary, we must acknowledge that the attitude of the trainer and the trainee is important in achieving successful results.

Volunteers (trainees) must be coachable. In other words, they must open their minds to be trained. A wonderful example of this occurred in 1985 when several recording stars came together to record "We Are The World" to raise funds for needy people in Africa. A sign by the entrance to the studio asked them to check their egos when they came in to the studio. The session would probably not have been a success unless they had complied and accepted training from the producer.

The leadership of the organization must make a commitment to train for long term success. The organization can not allow a leader to sacrifice the long term success of the organization for his short term success. His impact on the organization will not only be measured by his term of office, but by the success of his successor who he is responsible for training.

Recognize three things when training people:

1. There is no such thing as a dumb question, just dumb answers.

   People are often afraid to ask a question becuse they are treated like they are an idiot for not already knowing the answer. Welcome questions and treat even the silliest ones with the most respect. This will encourage people to ask questions and improve their performance.

2. How are they supposed to know if you do not tell them. Do not assume that someone will know what to do in a given situation. If you expect them to act in a specific manner, train them how to act in that situation.

3. How do you know they have learned what you have taught them, if you do not ask them after you have told them? Proper training is not a one way communication. People learn at different speeds. To conclude a successful training program, make sure that they have learned what you have taught them and not just heard what was presented.

We will address training the board of directors, prospective board members and activity chairmen. We will also discuss protocol, parliamentary procedure and personal improvement.

BOARD TRAINING

Training your board to be effective leaders is a year long task. It is the key to your success. If the board of directors is not properly trained, it will not be successful in executing its responsibilities and therefore the organization will not be successful.

The following techniques can be used to successfully train your board of directors:

- **Pre-Board Survey**—Conducting a survey will inform you of the experience of each of your new board members. This will help you to plan your training program for the year. Remember that each person will have different needs for training.

  (See the Pre-Board Survey segment in the planning section for further details).

- **Talk With Their Predecessors**—Have each new board member work with his predecessor during the transition period. This will teach each the current status of his area of responsibility. If the predecessor has a negative attitude toward the job or organization, do not allow him to brainwash the new board member.

- **Talk With Past Leaders Of The Organization**—Past leaders will have a broader perspective of the organization and its objectives. Their "old" ideas may be able to be used again as "new" ideas.

- **Train Prior To Your Annual Board Retreat (Planning Session)**— This training session may include parliamentary procedure, organization policies, etc. and will save time in your board retreat and board meetings.

- **Annual Board Retreat**—In addition to planning your annual goals and activities, this meeting is an excellent area to train your new board. Training can include:

  A. Notebook—Include everything the new board member will need to execute his responsibilities. Items you may wish to include are:

- Written job specifications
- Organization Constitution and/or By-Laws
- Long Range Plan
- Previous Annual Plan
- Organization Membership Roster
- Board of Directors Roster
- Calendar
- Budget
- Forms

B. Training Sessions—Training sessions at the board retreat are another opportunity to train the entire board together. Topics may vary according to your organization.

C. Speakers—Past presidents or other organization leaders may be utilized for training or motivational talks.

- **Board Meetings**—Training sessions or motivational speakers after board meetings can be helpful. If your board meetings are lengthy, reserve this technique for special occasions.

- **Planning Retreats**—When you conduct your quarterly or semi-annual retreats to monitor and evaluate your annual plan, schedule training based on the progress of the board to that date.

- **One-On-One**—As a leader, plan the training needs of the people who report to you and meet with them regularly to present one on one training that will supplement the training that is offered to the entire board.

- **Outside Training—Encourage your board members to attend motivational courses, speakers and other programs that will help their performance.**

- **Successor Training**—Toward the end of a board members' term of office, encourage him to motivate other members to run for his office. He should "mentor" the member and train him to insure his success.

PROSPECTIVE BOARD TRAINING

Organizations often have the problem of people who are elected to their board of directors who do not realize what they are getting into.

A training program for prospective board members will minimize this occurance and maximize your organization's effectiveness.

Have a program or reception before your nomination committee meets. This will save the nomination committee from having to consider candidates who find that they are no longer interested.

Have current office holders attend to answer questions about their responsibilities.

Potential presidential candidates and the president should encourage prospective board members to attend and discuss possible offices for the candidates to seek based on their knowledge of the candidate and the organization. The presidential candidates can also use this to start thinking about putting together their "team" (board).

PARLIAMENTARY PROCEDURE

Training your board and membership to utilize parliamentary procedures will make your meetings more productive and efficient. It will also minimize divisiveness within the organization by insuring majority rule while respecting the rights of the minority and the individual.

Parliamentary procedure pre-authorizes rules of organizing agendas and discussions of items of business. These rules eliminate the possibility of personalities or one side of an issue making rules to oppress a minority side or an individual the opportunity to have his views considered.

Although many books are available on the subject, conducting periodic training sessions on the rules and strategies of parliamentary procedure are suggested.

Most members will not read a book on parliamentary procedure so it is advisable to print a brief summary of the rules. A one-page table showing the most important motions, if it requires a second, if you can interrupt a speaker, if it is debatable, the required vote and other motions that may apply can help even the most inexperienced person learn the rules quickly.

Within the established rules, individuals or groups should plan strategies to maximize the probability that they convince a majority of the group to side with them on an issue. If an issue is on the published agenda, the member can lobby others before the meeting to vote with him on an issue. Lining up of your votes will prevent being railroaded by the other side, who has lined up their votes. If an issue is added to the agenda, you may wish to move to recess the meeting or adjournment until you can learn the feelings of the other members on the issue.

Other strategies to consider are who will speak on the issue, the sequence he will speak, who will make the motion, who will second the motion and who will call the question to end debate. Planning these strategies will make your presentations more efficient and may draw the undecided votes to your side.

Try to anticipate what the other side of the issue will do so that you can plan contingent strategies. If a surprise surfaces, you may want to try to table the motion, recess, adjourn or have your followers leave the meeting to eliminate a quorum to delay a vote on the motion.

(See conducting "Effective Board Meetings" in the personnel management section for additional tips for the organization president).

ACTIVITY MANAGEMENT

Volunteer activity chairmen are important to an organization not only for their contribution on the activity they chair, but they are the most likely future leaders of the organization.

The board member responsible for supervising the chairman begins training him with a one-on-one discussion where he will delegate the responsibility and authority for the activity using the delegation rules discussed in the personnel management section. Next, train the chairman to write a written activity plan using the rules discussed in the planning section.

During the execution of the activity plan, the activity chairman and responsible board member will extend the delegation and training process to each of the activity sub-chairmen and participants.

PROTOCOL

A volunteer organization often invites speakers and other dignitaries to visit its activities. The proper use of protocol will insure a favorable impression and successful event. Proper protocol steps are:

- Invite the guest as early as possible to maximize the probability that he will be able to attend.

- Send the guest a written invitation to minimize the chance that an oral invitation will be forgotten.

- Have something for him to do. An outside speaker will speak. Make sure that organization VIP's from other cities are used to speak, train, recruit new members and/or promote the organization through a press conference.

- Designate a host (couple) for each guest. This individual or couple will be available to make the guest's visit as comfortable as possible.

- Send a confirmation letter to the guest. Include details of the visit and what you would like the guest to do.

- Pay for everything.

- Seat the guest at the head table (if appropriate).

- Give him a proper introduction. Introduce him by rank of office (i.e. national, state, local, etc.). Have him supply an introduction if possible.

- Give him a standing ovation. Make him feel welcome!

- Give him a gift. A gift doesn't have to be expensive, but be special to your group. It is also nice to personalize the gift if you are aware of your guest's interests.

- Write a "THANK YOU NOTE" **that day.** This is a very special personal gift that costs nothing and is often forgotten. It will set you apart from the majority of other groups that the VIP guest will visit.

PERSONAL IMPROVEMENT

Depending on the experience of your members, you may want to offer personal development programs and or encourage your members to attend outside seminars and programs to enhance their management skills.

Seven topics that will develop the skills of your members and benefit your organization are:

- **Goal Setting**—Properly setting goals and rewarding their achievement will benefit everyone, and assist you in leading the organization to achieving your goals.

- **Leadership Skills**—People who are put into positions of leadership need to be aware of the alternative styles of leadership (i.e. autocratic, democratic, etc.). They can then formulate their own style based on the situation and the organization.

- **People Skills**—Every organization is made up of people, and the better you understand what motivates them and their personality styles, the better leader you will be. As an example, people in the accounting profession are usually more concerned with details and financial matters, whereas sales people usually look at things in a more conceptual manner and think of how to best market an idea.

(Additional information in the "Individual Volunteer" segment adds to this discussion).

- **Time Management**—We all have the same 24 hours in a day, 7 days in a week and 365 days in a year. The most often used excuse given by people for not volunteering is that they "Do Not Have Enough Time." People have to be taught how to expand their time. The cliche, "If You Need Something Done, Ask The Busiest Person You Know," demonstrates that the busiest and most successful people have learned to maximize their time.

Techniques that will expand your time include:

  - **Calendar**—Encourage your members to use a personal calendar. Take the time to show them how to efficiently use it for the organization and their business. Have them enter all organization activities from the organization's annual calendar into their personal calendar. List all major activities from the community in their calendar also. These listings in addition to their business appointments will help them maximize their time and eliminate double booking appointments or planning activities that compete against other major activities in the community.

- **Breakfast Meetings**—In addition to meeting after work or at lunch, breakfast meetings can add several hundred productive hours to your schedule every year.

Once people become accustomed to meeting early in the morning, they often prefer it because they can take care of business before normal daily disruptions occur.

- **Card System**—Card systems on the market such as the "Executive ScanCard System" offer you a method to separate activities and sub-activities for efficient management. Details are put on a card by subject and filed in a notebook that has shingled pockets so you can see the title of every card in the notebook at one glance. The cards are usually 3" x 3" to 3" x 5". This allows you to select the topic you need almost instantaneously. Notes can be written on a subject anytime that subject is thought about, which eliminates transferring notes from a notebook to a file later. Use one card per person you supervise and list all the subjects that you need to follow-up on with that person. Update the card as items are accomplished or added.

● **Communication Skills**—Everyone needs to be able to effectively communicate. Two important skills that will help your members are listening and writing skills.

- **Listening**—An often overlooked skill that is imperative for leaders is the skill of effective listening. The knowledge of how to work with people is ineffective if the person doesn't understand what a member is really saying.

- **Writing**—This includes communicating to people outside the organization and writing of the accomplishments of the current year to be used by future members in managing the organization.

- **Presentation/Speaking Skills**—Effective leaders must know how to speak, lead a meeting and present their organization to others. Many experts believe that an individual's probability of success is directly related to their skills to speak in public.

- **Computer Skills**—With the proliferation of personal computers, many organizations and individuals are using them in their volunteer efforts. Seminars on purchasing, programming and using personal computers will benefit your members and your group.

ADMINISTRATION

"There are only two kinds of people in the world. People who think they can and people who think that they can't, and they are both right."

Mark B. Yarnell

CONSTITUTION, BY-LAWS AND POLICIES

Every organization needs to have written laws and policies. Establishing a constitution, by-laws and or policies is one of your first items of business. You may compose all three documents or two based on the needs of your organization. The guidelines provided for in these rules minimize the possibility that an ineffective or domineering leader or individual can have from inflicting long term damage to the organization.

The constitution and by-laws are the major rules of the organization. Both of these documents should require a vote of the membership for amendment. Requiring a two thirds vote of a prescribed quorum will make amending these documents more difficult, and thus make the organization more stable. The constitution provides the backbone for the law of the organization and is the least specific of all three documents. By-laws are more detailed than the constitution, but still require a vote of the membership for an amendment. Amending one or both of these documents by a referendum initiated by the members may benefit your organization. Topics covered would include: name of the organization, affiliation(if any), purpose, membership, government, elections, appointment and recall, meetings, definitions, dues, activities, powers and duties of board members, rules of order, delegations, referendum and amendment.

Policies are usually pre-determined rules that are made by the board of directors and can be amended by the board at any meeting. After a newly elected board is installed, it ratifies the existing policies with any appropriate amendments. These rules are more specific and detailed than the rules in a constitution or by-laws. Topics can be established based on the needs of your organization. You may have a more detailed explanation of a topic that is in your constitution or by-laws or you may have have a topic that is not included in those documents.

ORGANIZATION STRUCTURE

The structure and duties of the board of directors are specified in your constitution and by-laws.

The size of your board is based on the size of your membership. Tying board size to membership size in your by-laws will permit you to adjust your board size without having to amend your by-laws.

Create a chart (see the example on the next page) showing each board position. The president or chairman is at the top of the chart. He supervises no more than 10 officers. Officers include vice-presidents (they may be differentiated by area of responsibility), the secretary, the treasurer, and other officers based on your needs. Each officer will have one to five directors report to him for assistance in the execution of their duties. Each director will have the appropriate activity chairmen and committees report to him. The legal counsel, chaplain, paid staff, and the immediate past president directly report to the president. The president and all officers comprise the executive committee.

Responsibilities for each board member are also included in your by-laws, but they can be supplemented by direction of the president. Like your paid staff, this communicates what performance is expected and gives the supervising officer a benchmark for evaluating that performance. Assign each board member a specific area of responsibility (i.e. Fundraising, Public Relations, etc.) for his term. This makes the board member more efficient because he learns from his experiences and will become more proficient.

Your by-laws will set the term of office for each board member. Some organizations stagger the term of office to provide a continuity of experienced leadership. Other organizations elect every position simultaneously. They rely on the use of board experience requirements as a qualification to run for office to provide the continuity of experienced leadership. The by-laws also specifies all offices available for presidential appointment.

Standing committees may be specified in the by-laws or be established as necessary by the president. Areas that standing committees are useful include: finance, by-laws, insurance and paid staff compensation. Have an odd number of members, with an executive committee member serving as the chairman. The president serves as an ex-officio member on all committees.

ORGANIZATION CHART

The samples illustrate two alternative examples of an organization chart. The first is basic and includes three individuals. The second is for a larger organization. Many varieties can be designed off of either of these examples.

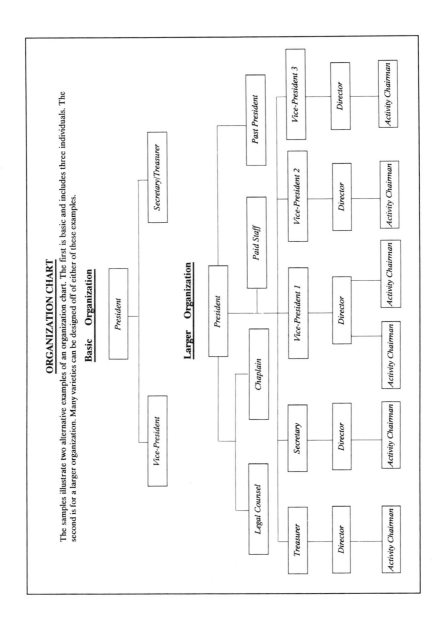

Basic   Organization

President

Vice-President

Secretary/Treasurer

Larger   Organization

President

Legal Counsel

Chaplain

Paid Staff

Past President

Treasurer

Secretary

Vice-President 1

Vice-President 2

Vice-President 3

Director

Director

Director

Director

Director

Activity Chairman

Activity Chairman

Activity Chairman

Activity Chairman

Activity Chairman

Activity Chairman

PAID STAFF

As your organization grows, it may become necessary to hire paid employees. As in business, establish policies to protect the organization and the employee.

The two basic duties of the paid staff are marketing or fundraising and administration. The size of your organization will dictate the number of part time and full time positions that you can afford.

Administrative assistants or secretaries are primarily employed for executing administrative duties. Their tasks can include answering the phone, opening and distributing the mail, taking minutes of meetings, maintaining and distributing membership rosters, maintaining membership files and billing dues, assisting the treasurer in financial matters and other duties as assigned by the president.

An executive director (or other appropriate title) is usually responsible for supervising the administrative staff and fundraising by soliciting corporate sponsorships. If you can not justify a full time executive director, try to find a person that may be the executive director for a group of small organizations. That provides you a part time employee, but someone who is a skilled professional.

Give all employees their job responsibilities in writing. This not only provides them a feeling of comfort by knowing what they are supposed to do, but gives the president and board of directors a benchmark to evaluate their performance.

Paid staff reports to and is supervised by the president only! The president approves and assigns all responsibilities, and is the sole source of any disciplinary measures. Allowing other board members to vary from this practice will cause problems with your board of directors and with the staff member.

Hiring—Firing—Compensation

- **Hiring**—It is the president's responsibility to interview candidates and recommend prospective employees for board approval. Appointment of a committee to assist the president has the following advantages.
  - Inclusion of potential future presidents will help insure the long term stability of the organization.
  - Past Presidents can offer experience and ideas that they learned from past mistakes and successes.

- **Firing**—After all other avenues have been tried and the board has decided to dismiss an employee, the president (only) should take care of this responsibility. Treat him the way you would like to be treated and be sensitive to his feelings.

- **Compensation**—Review employee performance regularly. Communicate results of each review and have the board approve all recommended actions. Use of year end bonuses in addition to raises will provide incentives to the employee without setting long term pay precedents. Establish policies regarding vacations and benefits and review them annually.

OFFICE

Establishing an office offers your organization several benefits.

- It increases the visibility of your organization in the community. It also adds to your credibility when you request donations or recruit members because people believe that you will exist tomorrow.
- It provides you a facility for maintaining your records.
- Depending on the size of the office, you can conduct membership, board and or committee meetings. This is more convenient and less expensive than using outside facilities.
- It gives you a facility for conducting at least some of your activities.
- Acts as a communication center. This gives you a permanent location for your telephone, computer, copier, records, telephone answering machine and for receiving mail.
- It provides a location for your members to informally gather to discuss organization business.

Owning your office is preferred, but may not be an option for you. If not, attempt to obtain the donation of an office by a business or another entity. If a donation is unavailable, try to lease an office at a discount rate. Another method to justify buying your own office is to rent it to other groups for meetings and activities. Make sure to compare the amount of existing meeting facilities in the community in relation to the demand before you make an investment based on this reason.

When you design the space for your office, list and prioritize every type of space requirement that you currently have or can anticipate.

Types of space you may require include:

- Secretary's office
- President's office
- Storage area
- Library—Records storage
- Awards Display area
- Board Room

- Membership meeting room—This can also be used for conducting the organization's activities.
- Restrooms
- Kitchen—Permits you to prepare refreshments and meals in-house.
- Social area

Work with a space planner to design the most useful space configuration. Try to design the facility so some of the rooms can be utilized for multiple functions. Removable partitions can allow you to have one large room that can be used for membership meetings or activities, and that can be divided into multiple rooms for committee or board meetings.

LEGAL COUNSEL

Appointing an attorney to be your legal counsel and represent your organization is imperative to minimize your exposure to any legal problem. In addition, your legal counsel can advise you concerning several areas of the organization's business.

The first area that an attorney can benefit your organization is in the writing of your constitution, by-laws and policies.

Next, contact the Secretary of State or other appropriate office in your state to apply for incorporation. The major benefit of incorporating your organization is that it limits the personal liability of your board of directors.

Once you have incorporated, have your legal counsel investigate the opportunity for you to apply for tax exempt status. First, apply to the IRS for income tax exemption, which may take several months to receive. After the IRS has given you approval, apply with your state for exemption of all appropriate taxes.

You may want to establish a 501c3 foundation, which will permit you to solicit tax deductible contributions. This will be discussed in more detail in the finance section, but is more difficult to qualify for than is the tax exempt status.

Have your legal counsel work with your treasurer to insure that you comply with all regulations regarding your submission and maintenance of financial records.

Appoint your legal counsel to be a member of your insurance committee to assure that the organization is properly covered with liability insurance.

Finally, your legal counsel should approve all contracts **before** they are signed and represent the organization in any legal matter.

ELECTIONS

Some organization's boards of directors are elected by the membership and others are nominated and elected by a nominating committee. I will address the procedure for nominating, campaigning and being elected to office in this volume. Other methods can be adapted based on the needs of your organization.

Electing your board of directors strengthens your organization because:

- It creates excitement within the organization.
- Involving all of your members in the process will draw them closer together as a group.
- Going through a public nomination and election process will reaffirm the commitment of the people elected, to diligently serve the organization.

Having contested races demonstrates that the offices sought are prestigious and that several people are interested in serving the organization. People also appreciate their election to an office more if they had to defeat a respected co-worker than if they won an uncontested race.

Your constitution and by-laws dictates your election procedures and qualifications to hold office. Requiring varying amounts of previous experience in the organization will insure that you have qualified candidates run for office. You might require presidential candidates to have served on the board of directors for two years with one year as an officer. Vice-presidents may have had to serve on the board for six months and directors may only be required to have been a member for X months. This will also minimize the opportunity that a poor leader will be elected.

I do not recommend electing a president-elect when you elect your president. This eliminates motivation for that person and other people during the ensuing term. He also can coast to save his energies and ideas until his term begins. Advocates of this method say that it allows that person to be trained for the presidency. My feelings are that if the organization is training its leaders properly two or three candidates would be qualified to run for president and electing him one full term early may discourage the others from continuing their participation in the organization.

Plan your elections at the annual planning retreat. Once the election date has been set, plan all other activities by back dating them on the calendar to allow adequate time for conducting and meeting any requirements in your by-laws.

The election process has four phases, which we will detail below:

Nomination of Candidates

Establish a nominating committee with the immediate past president as chairman. Other members should include other past presidents, past officers and current board members who do not plan to run for office.

Their duty is to present a ballot of qualified candidates to the membership for them to elect the new board of directors.

Their first task is to solicit nominees from the membership. It can be done by mailing a nomination letter to the membership or inserting it into your newsletter. Current and past leaders should not only nominate people, but they should motivate those people to run for office.

Once the nominations have been received, the chairman of the nomination committee contacts all people who were nominated. Some will decline the nomination, some will be excited and some will want to know more information before they decide to run for office.

As we discussed in the training section, a prospective board training meeting will provide the necessary information about the responsibilities of each office. It will also save the nominating committee time and provide you with more qualified candidates.

Next, the nominating committee will meet to interview all prospective candidates. This responsibility is twofold. First, they must verify that the candidate meets all requirements to run for the office that he desires. Second, they look between the lines to make sure that the person is dedicated to the organization and consider if he may be better suited for another office. Upon completion of the interviews, they will submit a ballot to the membership for consideration. A method of running for office if a person is not included on the ballot for one reason or the other should be considered. He may miss the interview process or may want to run for a higher office than the nominating committee certified him to run for.

Campaigning for Office

Once we have nominated candidates, the official campaign season begins. You will always have people who will campaign year round, but it can be as detrimental as beneficial to their candidacy.

It is very important that the candidates for office not jeopardize the current year's achievements by directing all of their efforts toward their campaign. The current president must be watchful for this and minimize its negative effects.

Candidates for office may utilize a variety of techniques to enhance their odds for election. Personal letters to the entire membership, phone calls to the members and hosting campaign parties are a few successful techniques. Printing resumes, campaign literature and posters are old favorites that are good and create excitement.

One technique that will minimize the amount of time individual candidates spend campaigning is to hold a political bash. This is a party where every candidate has a booth with food or drink set up at the same time. The organization sponsors the event and invites the entire membership. It not only gives members the opportunity to talk with all of the candidates at one time, but offers an opportunity for all members to socialize and enjoy their involvement in the organization.

The Election Meeting

Promote the election meeting as the biggest meeting of the year. It can be held during a regular membership meeting or at a special meeting time. Mailouts and phone calls to the membership, in addition to hotly contested races will encourage a large attendance. Offer free refreshments with the candidates buying the refreshments as a filing fee and you will increase your attendance also.

Set up a table by the front door with a membership roster available. As members walk into the room, verify him as a member, have him sign a sign-in sheet and issue him a ballot. If you have a large membership, you may want to split your roster to permit more people to work the table. If candidates have not paid their fee, it should be collected at this time.

The chairman of the nominating committee presides at the meeting. Responsibilities include introducing speakers, calling for ballots to be collected and working with the committee to count the ballots to insure a fair election.

Offices are elected one at a time starting with the president. This allows a qualified candidate to drop down to the next race if he loses the race for which he was nominated. A pre-determined amount of time is allowed for each candidate and anyone that he may wish to speak for him to make a presentation on behalf of his candidacy. The amount of time is normally the longest for president and decreases for the executive offices and board members.

After all speeches are given for one position, the chairman will call for ballots to be collected and tabulated. Print all the races on one form and ask that the members tear off the appropriate portion for each race. Allow blank spaces for write-in and drop down candidates and have a few blank sections on the form in the event of a run-off or a tie. If there is an uncontested race, the chairman should solicit a motion to elect the candidate by acclamation.

Once all the elections are concluded, the meeting can be used as a social event and the winning and losing candidates can shake hands and turn to the primary business, which is improving the organization and their community.

Transition

The time from the election of a new board until it takes office can be very critical to the organization. It is again important, not to sacrifice the success of the current administration by turning all of the efforts to the new term.

Encourage newly elected officers to work with their predecessors to determine current status of the office. This is also an excellent method of training the new officers.

The new president sends a letter to all of the new board members advising them of the critical dates of meetings, training sessions, etc. that they should attend. It also advises them of the upcoming job responsibilities and welcomes them to the president's team.

A joint board meeting of the old and new board of directors provides another method of training the new board of its position and the current status of the organization. It also provides an informal time for the two groups, and is usually the last time that the old board of directors will meet as a group.

RECORDS

Maintaining good records on the organization and its business is essential to it being successful. It can also provide interesting historical information.

If you have an office, the records can be filed at the office or in an off-site storage. If you don't have an office, the records can be passed from administration to administration and kept at the president's home or office and the remainder kept in off-site storage.

Contact your public library. Ask them if they would like you to donate past annual reports, newsletters and other documents that would complement its historical collections for the community.

The most important records are the organizations's financial statements and tax records that are required by law. A Certified Public Accountant should advise you about the submission, requirements, and the length of time that these records be kept by the organization.

Other records you should maintain include:

- **Current Membership**—This provides you the name, address and phone number for communicating information about the organization and its activities.

- **Past Members**—Although they are not currently active members, these people can re-join, donate money, donate goods or services, or refer new members to the organization.

- **Past Annual and Activity Plans**—In addition to historical information, they can help you better manage the organization and its activities in the future.

- **Meeting and Board Meeting Agendas and Minutes**—Provide excellent information that can substantiate what happened in the past and why it happened.

- **Publications**
  - **Annual Reports**—Reflect the history of the group by year.
  - **Newsletters**—Provide more detail and cover a shorter time span than the annual report.
  - **Photographs**—Label all photographs. They might be valuable in the future. A past member may become famous or they can be viewed at reunions.

- **Awards**—Improve morale and create pride in the organization. It is said that "success breeds success." Past achievements can be a motivational tool.

- **Audio and Video Tapes**—Meetings, activities, interviews with past presidents about their administration, etc. can provide you with an excellent supplement to your written history.

- **Historical Information**—This can be anything from flags, furniture, items donated by past members, etc. that has a value to the history of the organization.

PERSONNEL

MANAGEMENT

"The final test of a leader is that he leaves behind him in other men the conviction and the will to carry on."

Walter Lippman, **Roosevelt Has Gone**

MEMBERSHIP

An organization can not function or survive without people. The recruitment, activation and retention of people or members in an organization requires three distinctly different management operations. It is advisable to divide your membership efforts into:

- **Membership Recruitment**—Like the sales department of a car dealership, their responsibility is to "sell" (recruit) as many people as possible to join the organization.

- **Activation**—Like the service department of the car dealership, their responsibility is to provide each member the activities that will satisfy their needs. If this department does not satisfy the needs of the members, the retention department will have a virtually impossible job.

- **Membership Retention**—Like the bookkeeping department at the car dealership, their responsibility is to make sure that the members continue their involvement by paying their dues. This group must work closely with the activation committee and work throughout the year. The retention committee will not be successful, if it only contacts the members at the time they collect membership dues.

100% membership retention is difficult, but retention activities help to locate members that the activaltion department may have missed and get them re-activated. It also helps resell marginally interested members in re-joining the organization.

Let's explore each of the areas and ideas to make them a successful part of your organization.

MEMBERSHIP RECRUITMENT

Why are new members the lifeblood of an organization? New members provide seven benefits to an organization. They include:

- **New ideas**—New members bring new ideas, which will help you be more successful.

- **Manpower**—Everyone always needs additional manpower. New members are fresh troops for your next activity.

- **Chairmen and committee members**—New members mean that the same tired member will not have to chair or serve on the committee year after year.

- **More service to the community or your constituency**—Having more people means you can conduct more activities and **impact more people.** This is what we're all trying to accomplish.

- **Conduct more and larger activities**—Some activities are so large and/or sophisticated that they can not be conducted without a large number of members.

- **Return the favor**—If you enjoy the organization, offer it to a friend. Give them the same opportunity that someone gave to you.

- **Insure the future of the organization**—Without new people, the organization will eventually die. A constant influx of new members will virtually insure that the organization will exist in the future.

Before discussing "how to" recruit new members into your organization, we must know what your membership goal is for the year.

MEMBERSHIP PLAN

Complete the membership plan at the annual board planning retreat. By setting a goal for the desired total membership at year end, and forecasting your retention percentage of existing members, you can forecast how many new members you must recruit to achieve your goal. The number of new members required helps you to plan the number, frequency and types of activities necessary to achieve the goal. The plan should be reviewed at board meetings and at the quarterly planning retreats to monitor, evaluate and revise the plan.

The formula for calculating your membership plan is:

YEAR END DESIRED MEMBERSHIP LEVEL

$-$ FORECASTED NUMBER OF MEMBERS RETAINED

$=$ NEW MEMBERS REQUIRED

Similar to cash flow management of a budget, the membership plan should be divided monthly, quarterly, etc. depending on your organization's memberships' dues cycles. This will allow you to manage the goal continuously.

If you are behind, you can add activities to recruit more new members or increase your retention percentage.

Now that the we know how many new members we want to recruit, we need to discuss "how to" recruit them.

HOW TO RECRUIT NEW MEMBERS

The following list of techniques contain examples of activities that will provide opportunities and motivation for your members to recruit new members.

- **Have a membership booth at your activities**—If you're selling hot dogs in a booth at the county fair, have membership information available. If you are sponsoring a large event, have a dedicated membership information booth set up.

- **Orientations**—As discussed in more detail later in this section, orientations are an excellent tool for recruiting new members in addition to educating existing members about the organization.

- **Membership meetings**—Also discussed in more detail in the personnel management section, a membership meeting should not only be utilized for communicating to existing members, but as an opportunity to show off the organization to guests and recruit them into the organization.

- **Membership blitzes**—A blitz can recruit a large number of new members in a very short time. It can be one day, a week, or a month long. A group of volunteers are organized to try to talk to as many people as possible during the blitz about joining the organization. Breaking the volunteers into teams and establishing a competition and awards for the most successful team provides better results and makes the blitz more fun for the volunteers.

- **Casino and other parties**—Using a social for a membership recruiting tool is very successful because the prospective member feels more comfortable in a social atmosphere.

  A casino party or Las Vegas night is where you gamble for "play money" and then bid for donated prizes. An incentive for members to bring guests and recruit members might be free admission, extra play money or one chance per guest brought and two chances per new member signed for a drawing for a highly desired prize.

Other parties include having a nightclub donate a free happy hour. The refreshments are usually free, so you want to make a big push to have as many people attend as possible.

- **Public Service Announcements**—This idea draws mixed results, but when used in conjunction with news about other activities that you're conducting will produce additional publicity and new members for your organization.

- **Ask your new members for referrals**—Like the insurance business, every time a new member joins the organization ask them to provide you the name of friend that might be a prospective member. Quite often new members are afraid to ask friends to join because if their friend doesn't like the organization they think they will be blamed. Just ask your new members for referrals, and then you and your experienced members can recruit them into the organization.

- **Contact past members for referrals**—A good but often overlooked source for prospective members are past members who enjoyed the organization, but are not active now. They can influence friends, employees, etc. who might experience the same benefits that they had. Be careful to ask a past member who had a positive experience with the organization.

- **Ask your board of directors to make a personal commitment to recruit X new members during the year.**—Your board members are the most committed members to the organization and should be your best recruiters.

- **Ask your entire membership to recruit at least one member during the year.** This is not a difficult task, and if you share the benefits of increased membership discussed earlier, you should have no problem convincing your membership of the importance of enlarging the organization.

- **Insert material into the "welcome new resident" kit**—New residents in your community are the best prospects for joining an organization. It provides them a quick start to meet their new neighbors in the community.

- **President's Team**—This incentive establishes an opportunity for your members to earn special recognition for recruiting members. Levels are established with corresponding members that have to be recruited to reach the level and what the reward is for that level. Several levels are offered so that everyone can participate. Your most aggressive recruiter will always have a higher goal to aim toward. To be successful, the team must be made prestigious so that everyone will aspire to belong to it. Also, the rewards for each level must be items that your membership would desire and commensurate with the difficulty in reaching that level.

- **Corporate sponsorships**—Discussed in further detail in the finance section, corporate sponsorships offer your organization the opportunity to recruit new members in addition to raising money. Offering the sponsors a number of memberships for their employees with their contribution provides you two benefits for the price of one.

- **Incentives**—We have discussed some incentives while discussing specific ideas previously, but it is critical enough to merit repeating again. Incentives, recognition and enthusiasm provide the motivation that will make your members become excited about recruiting new members.

Two methods of recruiting new members deserve more detail than was spent on the previously mentioned techniques. These are membership nights and one-on-one recruiting.

MEMBERSHIP NIGHTS

There are five steps to conducting a successful membership night. They are:

1. Thoroughly plan the activity using the activity planning procedure discussed previously in the planning section.

2. As a part of the activity plan, pay special attention to whom you are going to invite and how you will get them to attend the activity.

   - Whom will you invite?
     - Friends of your members. These people can be discovered in a variety of ways. One is to have an incentive membership meeting for the person who submits the most names of prospective members at the meeting. Incentives for the member who brings the most guests and recruits the most new members are also very effective.

— Referrals from past members.

— Referrals from corporate sponsors.

— Past prospective members who have not joined.

- How will you get them to attend the activity?

  — Send them an invitation. A professional invitation that tells the prospect that they have been "recommended" for membership is more effective than a postcard or photocopied flier. Include an RSVP to add importance to the invitation and help to give you an idea of how many are thinking about attending the event.

  — Follow-up calls a few days before the activity will help to persuade the prospects to attend.

  — Public service announcements advertising the event will attract some prospects.

  — Word of mouth. Your membership should be selling their friends on attending the event in response to your motivation and the incentives you have offered them.

3. The orchestration of the activity must occur without incident to portray the best possible image of your organization to your guests.

   - **Location**—The location should be easy to find, centrally located and provide ample parking. It is easy to lose an interested prospect if they have to drive too far, can not find a parking place or locate the building or room. Try to have a private room to avoid distractions.

   - **Name Tags**—Have name tags for your members and "guest" name tags for your guests. As each guest joins, have the recruiter cross off the "guest" on his name tag to inform other members that he has joined so that they can approach and recruit another guest.

   - **Refreshments**—Have some refreshments. If you are going to serve alcohol, make sure to comply with all laws. Also, make sure that you are properly insured and do not let anyone overindulge.

   - **Sales Desk**—This desk should be manned by informed members who will make sure everyone signs in his name and address, have organizational materials available, application forms, charge card forms and other materials as necessary. Turn all memberships into this desk so that an ongoing count of your progress can be kept.

- **Pick up the guests**—90% of the guests you pick up will join, but only 40% of the guests who come on their own join. This also makes sure that they attend.

- **Have a greeting committee**—It is their job to greet the guests upon arrival, to see that they feel comfortable, introduce other members and make sure they are not left unattended.

- **The Presentation area**—Make sure that the presentation area is smaller than you need. Set up fewer chairs as a crowded room appears better than an empty room. You can always add chairs. Make sure the microphone, sound system, slide projector and other equipment is functioning.

4. The presentation of your organization during the program must be well rehearsed and conducted.

- Have a written agenda. This will force you to plan every detail of your program. Do not let the program run more than 30-45 minutes. It is better to be too short than too long as you will lose the prospect's interest.

- Consider having an informal social time while everyone is arriving.

- Call the meeting to order, and begin by informing the group about your organization's purpose and activities.

- Have a VIP for a closing speaker. It is better if the speaker has been a member so they can sell the membership benefits from personal experience. Give the speaker explicit instructions on what you would like for him to say and how long he has to speak.

- Thank the speaker, ask everyone to join and adjourn for one-on-one discussions with the prospects about joining.

- Have a "Hit Team" of experienced members who will make sure that every guest is asked to join.

- Reconvene the meeting after a few minutes and introduce all the new members in front of the group. This peer pressure can easily result in a few additional new members.

- Do not formally adjourn the meeting, but step away from the microphone and continue to talk with prospects who did not join as long as possible.

5. Your job is not finished when the event is over.

- Follow up with the new members to make sure they attend your next meeting or activity.
- Follow-up on the ones who did not join. Invite them to your next activity and ask them to join again.
- Follow-up with the prospects who did not attend. Invite them to your next activity and invite them to join.
- Complete the implementation and evaluation portion of your activity plan and submit a final report to the board of directors.

ONE-ON-ONE RECRUITING

This method is used in nearly every technique discussed previously. It is important to train your members in how to recruit new members. If they have a few negative experiences, they may quit recruiting altogether. Here are some thoughts to remember when talking to a prospective member:

1. Respect his time—Too often, well meaning members try to tell a prospective member everything about an organization and either bore him to death or talk him out of joining after he was initially persuaded to join. The old adage, "Why say boo boo, when boo will do," is very appropriate here.

2. Mention what the organization does and why—Do not mention every activity, but find one early that he is interested in and use it to close the recruitment sale.

3. Tell him why he is needed in the organization—This should relate to his experience and interests. Help him to visualize how much better the organization will function with his help.

4. If he is a friend, ask him if he wants what you have?—Share your success stories of how the organization has helped you, and ask him if he could benefit from the same help.

5. **ASK HIM TO JOIN**—Too often, we do a great job telling the prospect about the organizaation, but we do not **ask him to join**! He can only say yes, no or maybe. If he says yes, congratulations! If he says no or maybe, then you need to ask him why as his negative response indicates that he need additional information. After he has given you his question, answer only

that question and then ask him to join again. He will either join, bring up another question or tell you why he really will not join.

Everyone is not going to join your organization when asked, but he will not join unless he is asked.

There are legitimate reasons for not joining, including that the time may not be right. Respect his answer, put him into a tickler file to call him in the future and do not create a negative image of your organization by reacting negatively to his answer.

OVERCOMING OBJECTIONS TO JOINING THE ORGANIZATION

Many objections may be given for not joining an organization, but the two heard most often are: I do not have enough time and it costs too much. Overcoming these objections will make the difference in a successful year of membership recruitment. Let's look at each of these objections and some possible answers to them:

- **I do not have enough time.** People can **always** make time for the things that they are interested in doing. Your job is to convince them that the organization is worthy of their time. When he raises this objection, ask him, what the organization would have to offer to be worthy of his time? Assure him that the time commitments are minimal and that his involvement will make a difference in the organization's success. The expression, "When you need a job done, ask the busiest person you know" is applicable because a busy person realizes that he can make a difference and learns how to manage his time more efficiently.

- **It costs too much**. When this objection is raised, offer him a time payment plan or use his credit card to pay his dues (if available). Also, add up the benefits of the organization in a dollar term to show the prospect that his dues will more than be paid back in benefits. Another technique is to divide the cost of the dues into a daily cost or relate it to another item (i.e. one cup of coffee per day).

You will not be able to convince everyone who raises these objections to join, but by being prepared for them and others that pertain to your organization, you will recruit more new members.

ACTIVATION

Once you have recruited a new member, your work to make him a valuable asset to your organization has just begun. An aggressive program to activate the members will help you involve the maximum number of members in your programs. Realize that no matter how well your activation team works, that you will never have everyone participate in an activity. Do not let this discourage you. Personal contact is the best medium for contacting members and encouraging their involvement. Making the organization and its activities **FUN** is very important, as it motivates members to participate.

There are 10 steps to activate or reactivate a member. They are:

1. **Make the new member feel wanted and needed.**
   - All members should approach each new member, shake his hand and welcome him to the organization.
   - Assign each new member a "mentor" (experienced member) who is responsible for helping the new member while he becomes oriented to the organization.
   - The president should mail a letter formally welcoming the new member to the organization.
   - If possible, the president should phone each new member within 48 hours of his joining to cordially welcome him to the organization.
   - Provide the new member a name badge, so he will feel like a member and not a new member.
   - List each new member in your organization's publication.
   - Submit new members' names to appropriate outside newspapers and other publications for additional recognition.

2. **Get to know the new member.**
   - Provide each new member a form that will provide personal information about him.
     - Birthday
     - Spouse's name
     - Children's name and age
     - Wedding date
     - Employer/job
     - Hobbies
     - Interests
     - Ambitions

- Make sure that at least one officer personally visits with the new member to discuss his interest in the organization and opportunities for his participation.

3. **Provide him an orientation about the organization.**(See orientation information later in this section.)

   - Invite his spouse if appropriate.

4. **Get him involved!**

   - As soon as possible recruit the new member to participate in an activity. If you wait, he will feel like he is not needed, and if this occurs, he will find an organization that will meet his need.

5. **Give him some responsibility.**

   - Ask the new member to bring a guest to an activity within 30 days. This tactic used successfully in the insurance business, will significantly increase your membership.

   - Ask him to serve as a sub-chairman or chairman of an activity.

6. **Do not use a new member or existing member only on fundraising or manual labor activities.**

   If the member feels that you only want him because he can raise money or do manual labor, burnout will occur, causing him to lose interest in participating in the organization's activities.

7. **Keep him informed about group activities.**

   - Give him a new member kit (This is detailed in the orientation segment).

   - Have a training program in place that will train new members about your organization.

   - 30/60/90 Program

     Have an activation committee phone the new member each 30 days after he joins to make sure that he knows about the activities and is receiving the organization's publications. A A different member of the committee should phone the member each month. This will also make the new member feel that he is wanted because the president, his montor and at least 3 other members have phoned him the first 90 days of his membership.

8. **Compliment and reward his performance.**

   - Like other members, the new member will be more likely to continue his involvement, if the organization recognizes his contributions. (See Awards and Incentives in this segment for a detailed discussion.)

9. **Keep up with the changes in his life.**

   - Maintain a tickler file with his biographical information.
     - Send wedding, anniversary and birthday cards.
     - Update the file at least annually.

10. **Continue to call him for help even after he has been unable or unwilling.**

    - Maintain an activity chart, so that you know immediately if the member has missed a pre-designated number of activities (i.e.—3).

    - If the member can not participate, he may contribute money, an idea or refer you to another person who will help on the activity.

MEMBERSHIP RETENTION

A good activation program, as previously discussed, that activates a new member early is the best retention tool. It will provide the activities that interest the member and that will keeps him involved.

The effort to retain a member must begin as soon as he joins. If you wait until his membership renewal is due, he will not respond to your request that he maintains his membership. He will have found an organization or another activity to give of his precious time.

Establish a special retention committee whose job will be to conduct special activities targeted to maximize your membership retention. Four of these activities are:

- 90/60/30 Plan
  Similar to the 30/60/90 plan discussed in the activation segment, this plan will have different members call the member every 30 days for the 90 days before his membership is up. This makes sure that the member knows about upcoming activities. The first caller should not mention that his membership is about to expire. The second caller should invite him to an activity and gingerly inquire about his continued membership. If the member does not come to either of these activities, he is not a likely candidate to renew his membership. The third caller should firmly ask him to renew his membership and then invite him to an activity. If he says no, do not argue. Give his name to the organization president or a close friend who is a member. A call from either of these two people may change his mind.

- Send the member his first dues bill 60 days before his membership expires. The members who renew from this notice will not require any efforts from the retention committee. This will free the committee to work on the members who are less likely to renew their membership. Send the member a thank you letter as soon as he renews his membership.

- Send the member his second dues bill 30 days before his membership expires.

- Put the number of years that a member has been in the organization on his name tag. This will create another level of pride and prestige. Give special awards to members who attain milestones in length of membership (i.e. 5, 10, 15, etc. years).

BUILDING A SUCCESSFUL TEAM

No leader can do everything in an organization. The leader must have people to lead, and to be successful, he must mold his people into a team. There are six steps to building a successful team. They are:

- **Establish a common goal.**

  Everyone must proceed to a common end. The common goal is the glue that holds the members together. In World War II, America's goal was to win the war and insure our freedom. Once you have a common goal, you are now ready to establish your annual plan.

  Create a theme to describe your goal or the year ahead. When I was a president of a Jaycee chapter, I wanted a theme to demonstrate that our chapter was totally committed, regardless of the costs, to being the very best chapter it could be. Our theme was:

  > "Fixed Bayonets
  > Take No Prisoners
  > Shoot The Wounded and
  > Eat The Horses"

- **Train your team.**

  As the leader, you must have a vision of what it will take for you to accomplish your goal. You must develop a training program that will prepare your members to accomplish the tasks necessary to achieve that goal.

- **Provide your team constant communications.**

  Provide your team feedback on your progress. Ask them their opinion on issues. This will reaffirm their commitment to the team's goal.

- **Be enthusiastic at all times!**

  As the leader, you can not be negative about anything. Negativism is too prevalent as it is, and your negativism will create doubt about your ability to achieve your goal among your team.

- **Execute your plan.**

  The team must focus on executing the plan, since it contains the necessary tasks to accomplish your organization goal.

  Delegating responsibilities and following-up to insure their accomplishment are the prime cornerstones to insure the realization of your organization's goal.

- **Recognize, reward and motivate your team.**

  You can not recognize and reward those who give their all to your organization enough. The more you reward your team for their work, the more work they will do.

  Encourage your members to become involved in as many activities as possible. Be mindful of their interests and ambitions. If you help your team members achieve their goals in the organization, they will help you to achieve your goals as the leader of the organization.

- **Evaluate your plan.**

  Monitor your plan at every board meeting and with quarterly planning retreats. This will help you to insure that you maintain the proper direction toward achieving your goal.

ORIENTATIONS

Orientations are an important event that can be used to educate, activate, reactivate your members and recruit more new members into your organization.

Planning an orientation program is critical to its success, because you usually only have one opportunity per member or prospective member to sell the organization and its activities at an orientation.

Remember the following points when you are planning your orientation program:

- **Conduct your orientation programs regularly.** Once a month is preferred, but once a quarter is minimal. This allows you more opportunities to sell your organization. People like routines. If you're membership is actively recruiting new prospective members, it is easier for them to invite the prospect to an orientation if it is conducted every first Tuesday, than if they never know when the next orientation will be held.

- **The primary purpose of the orientation is to sell members and prospective members on getting actively involved in the organization.**

- **Include the history of the organization in the orientation.** Knowledge of organizational history adds credibility to the organization and instills pride in your membership.

- **Discuss the current activities of the organization.** The prospective member is looking for something of interest. If you offer a program that draws his interest, he will join and become active.

The agenda of the orientation must be well planned. Do not make it too long as it is imperative to obtain their interest, bring it to a peak and STOP (YES STOP) while they are ready to buy. Always leave them wanting more information. A sample agenda for an orientation looks like this:

6:30 p.m.   Introduction of attendees

6:33 p.m.   Purpose of organization

6:36 p.m.   Discuss the activities that are conducted locally.

6:45 p.m.   How the member or prospective member can help.

6:50 p.m.   Closing speech (President or VIP)

6:55 p.m.   Questions and Answers

7:00 p.m.   One-on-one visiting with attendees to recruit them as members and activity committee members.

The image of your organization you portray to the attendee is also dependent on the techniques of your presentation. Techniques include:

- **Slides or Videotape**—The old saying that "a picture is worth a thousand words" is so true. Select pictures that show the activities and that the people participating are having **FUN**. Include as many of your members in the presentation as possible. Everyone likes to see his picture on the big screen, and he will be more likely to bring guests if he is included.

- **President or VIP Speech**—Most guests will appreciate the organization's president or VIP who takes time from his schedule to share his love of the organization with new or prospective members. It is important that he stays after their speech to meet the attendees and personally recruit their involvement.

- **New Member Kit**—This is for new members and not for prospective members. The new member kit is one more reason for a guest to join. It shows the concern of the organization for the new member and the prospective member sees it as an additional benefit of joining. Contents of the new member kit will vary by organization, but might include:
  - Membership Roster
  - List of the Board of Directors
  - Latest organization publication
  - List of activities of the organization
  - Calendar of upcoming events
  - Organization Chart
  - New Member Survey
  - A written history of the organization
  - Membership Pin
  - Corporate Sponsorship information—This will encourage some new members to solicit their employer for contributions on behalf of the organization.

- **Prearranged New Member**—This is where you already have an individual ready to join who attends the orientation and joins as soon as the presentation is over. This person will "break the ice" and make it easier for others to feel comfortable about joining. This tactic can also be utilized at membership recruitment functions.

MOTIVATING YOUR MEMBERSHIP

Motivating people can be frustrating in a volunteer environment because you can not use money or job security. These are the two most used motivational tools used in the business world, which can not be used in a volunteer organization. You must find other techniques to motivate your members. In the business world people will act if they are motivated enough even though it may cost them a raise or their job. This proves that money and job security are not the only things that motivate people.

First we should be aware of the qualities necessary to motivate people. They include:

- Ask the person you are motivating for his advice and involvement. People will not always volunteer until you ask them. Asking for his advice will make him feel needed and justify his involvement.

- Give him a reason to get involved. People will become involved if they feel that their involvement will make a difference. The reason that voter turnout is so low is that people do not feel that their vote will make a difference so they will not waste their time to vote. They will normally respond to a cause more than they will to the person unless you already are a friend.

- Listen to his ideas. When you ask for his advice, LISTEN. Fresh ideas can often be the best because the new person will not already have a bias about what needs to be done.

- Recognize people for their contributions. One of the reasons that people help is that they are looking for recognition. The more you recognize people for helping you, the easier it will be to recruit and motivate people to help you in the future.

- Be enthusiastic. Ralph Waldo Emerson said, "Nothing great was ever achieved without enthusiasm." Enthusiasm is contagious. If you are not excited about what you are doing, why should others be excited?

- Have goals. Having a goal gives people a yardstick to measure their performance. Seeing that they are contributing toward a goal that will help the organization will inspire them to additional contributions.

- Can do attitude. The saying that, "It's amazing what one can accomplish when one doesn't know what one can't do," describes the can do attitude. You must promote confidence in your people by letting them know that they can accomplish anything if they work hard enough.

- Get them involved. Delegate tasks to your members to get them involved. Again, you must make your members feel like their involvement will make a difference in the success of the activity.

How do you gather ideas and methods to motivate your members? Here are four examples that you can use:

- Learn from speakers and seminars. At these sessions, you will learn quotes and stories that you can adapt for your organization. (A list of favorite motivational quotes follows in the appendix).

- Use inspirational stories that you learn about from your newspaper, radio or television. Personalize these stories to your group.

- Learn from the experience of other people and organizations.

- Use your own experiences that you will adapt for the organization.

What motivates people to volunteer?

- Need to belong to a group.
- Want to accomplish something.
- Want to help their community.
- Want to meet people.
- Want to learn something new.
- A friend asked them to help.
- Recognition

AWARDS AND INCENTIVES

Why— TO REWARD AND MOTIVATE YOUR MEMBERS

- Reward—Everyone wants to be recognized for their volunteer efforts.
- Motivation—Members who observe others being recognized will want to know how they can receive an award. **DO NOT** forget this important motivational tool!

Who— EVERYONE WHO CONTRIBUTES TO THE **TEAM.**

How— BE CREATIVE

- Thank you notes—The best and most underrated award.
  — Write one per day minimum.
  — Handwrite the note yourself as it is more personal.
  — Thank him for his success and motivate him for additional participation in the organization.
  — Maintain a master file for future reference of who and when you wrote each thank you note. This can be helpful in determining future awards, nominees for officer positions and in other areas where a list of top performers will be beneficial.
- Certificates are an inexpensive award. They can be framed, or unframed.
- Plaques
- T-Shirts, caps and other inexpensive items.
- Trip and other more expensive awards can be offered for longer or more involved promotions.
- Challenges:
  — President offers a reward for a specified performance (i.e. Pie in the face of the President). As always the reward must stimulate a response to the challenge.
  — Divide your membership into teams led by board members. Have board members challenge other board members and their teams for who can recruit the most members, raise the most money, etc.
- President's Team—This should be established as a prestigious club, with a specific level of performance required to attain membership.

Key points to remember in this type of promotion are:
— Establish several levels of incentives. This gives the top achievers an almost endless opportunity to "cash in" on his achievements.
— You must offer rewards that your members want. The rewards should increase in value with each additional membership level.
— Promote the award regularly through announcements and presentations. Have special introductions of "team members" at meetings and list them in your publications.

● Name Tags offer a dual benefit to the organization. They can be offered as an award and they promote members meeting each other at functions.

● Send a letter to the winner's employer with a copy of your organization newsletter if appropriate. This is an excellent way to thank a member, motivate him for future participation and remind the employer of the good activities the organization performs in the community. The employer is a prospect for future sponsorships and allowing the employee to participate in future activities.

● OBTAIN DONATIONS whenever possible. Why pay for awards if you can obtain a donation?

When   —Present awards regularly so your members know when to expect presentations. You'll find members who increase their performance during a promotion period.

Meetings where awards can be presented include:
● Regular Membership Meetings
● Board Meetings
● Special Award Meetings
— Monthly
— Quarterly
— Annual Awards Banquet

PRESENTATION TECHNIQUES

● Make sure it is in public.

● It is showtime, so display your EXCITEMENT! As a leader you should be appreciative of the winner's contribution to the organization. Make sure everyone sees that appreciation in your presentation.

In the future, the memory of the award and its presentation will mean more than the certificate, plaque, trophy, etc.

- Take pictures to give to the recipient and use for promotional purposes.

IMPORTANT REMINDERS

- Keep politics out of the selection and presentation process. If politics become involved you will seriously damage the foreseeable future of your organization.

- If there is only one entry for an award, give it unless it does not meet the absolute minimal standards. The reward and motivation that come from the award will stimulate more and better quality entries in the future.

EFFECTIVE DELEGATION

No leader can accomplish every task in a successful organization. You need others to train to take your place as the leader and to help you achieve the organization's goals. As the old proverb says, "Many hands make work light." Once you have the people ready to help, you must exercise the "Art of Delegation" to improve on the performance of your organization. That's right, delegating is a learned art, not an inherited capability or a science.

One of the greatest causes for burnout and failure of volunteer leaders is that they do not recognize, have not learned how or are afraid to delegate responsibilities to others.

WHY DELEGATE ?

Here are six reasons:

- It allows the organization to accomplish more by having more people contribute to it.
- It allows the president to spend more time managing people and developing long range plans and less time on individual tasks.
- It increases the efficiency of your organization.
- It helps develop members for future leadership by teaching management and leadership skills.
- It creates enthusiasm among your members because they know that they are "making a difference" in the accomplishments of the organization.
- Your members will develop a feeling of responsibility for the organization, which will intensify their feelings toward the organization and their participation. Delegating to the lowest possible level will make everyone feel more a part of the team and make them more likely to volunteer for future responsibilities.

WHO SHOULD YOU DELEGATE TO ?

Now that you agree that delegating responsibility will enhance your organization, it is time to look at "whom" is the person you should delegate the responsibility.

Someone in your organization can do almost every individual job better than you.

To select the best person, you should:

- **Consider their interests and abilities.** An accountant may have more experience and be more interested in being a treasurer that he would raising funds or recruiting new members, etc. You are like a baseball manager and need to consider who would be the best outfielder or pitcher. Your ability to blend everyone's talents will produce a more successful team.

- **Ask yourself, how much will the job challenge them?**
  Do not give someone the same job all of the time. An example is asking someone to always raise funds or recruit new members. Also, most people will not be motivated to successfully execute a responsibility at a lower level in the organization than they have previously held. Once someone has been the president of the organization, they usually will not have the same desire they once had, if they become a board director or a vice-president.

- **Who needs the job the most?**
  Consider the goals and ambitions of your members. An individual who aspires to be president may benefit from a certain responsibility more than someone else. The president's responsibility is to develop the future leadership of the organization and this question will help them to successfully execute that responsibility.

- **Try to balance the opportunities delegated among your membership.** Be careful not to overload an individual because he has done a good job in the past. He may not be able to say no and eventually fail or burnout.

QUESTIONS YOU MUST ASK YOURSELF

Delegating a task gives others the authority to make decisions that are your ultimate responsibility. Before you delegate a responsibility, you need to look in the mirror and make sure you are ready to be an effective delegator. Ask yourself these questions:

- Other people have good ideas. Will you accept and properly credit others for their ideas?
- Everyone makes mistakes. Are you willing to accept the mistakes others make and train them to prevent the same

mistake in the future? It is important to maintain an even temper even during a distressful situation. If you lose your poise over small matters, it will limit your ability to find people who will accept your delegated responsibilities.

- People have different methods of doing a job. Are you more concerned with the results of a job than the methods used to complete the job? Let him do it his way! This encourages creativity and it makes the individual become more involved with the delegated activity. Restrain yourself from telling him how to do everything.

You need to be able to answer "yes" to the above questions. If you can not, do not give up, but work on these items.

HOW TO DELEGATE A RESPONSIBILITY

To effectively delegate a responsibility:

- **Establish a two way communication about the job ahead.**
  - **Discuss the intended results and priorities.**
  - **Tell him how much authority he has.** Once you have given him the authority, **do not** rescind or circumvent it unless there are extenuating circumstances. He will be waiting for you to "yank the rug out from under him," and when he sees that you will not do that, he will respect you and work harder to perform for you.
  - **Tell him the rules for executing his authority.** Try to give him a complete list, as any rules that arise during his execution of the activity might jeopardize its success, or, embarrass him and make you appear less effective as the leader.
  - **Stress the importance of the delegated activity.** Tell him how it contributes to achieving the overall goals of the organization.
  - **Take the time to communicate effectively.**
    Make sure that you both understand each other's responsibility to the delegated activity.
- **Establish goals for the delegated activity.**
  Let them offer their input. They may be more ambitious than you are and want to set a higher goal. Write the goals as part of a written activity plan.

- **FOLLOW UP, FOLLOW UP, FOLLOW UP**

  Some people have no problem delegating a responsibility, but then wonder why the activity is not successful. Too often, people delegate a task and then leave the person alone until the date it is supposed to be completed. When you delegate an activity, it does **not** release you from your ultimate responsibility for the activity. To effectively follow up on a task you have delegated:

  — **Insist on regular reports on the activity.** Regular reports will provide you with signs that will If the person does not you if the activity will be successful or not. follow through on the interim tasks, they are unlikely to complete their total responsibility.

  — **Respond appropriately to the realized progress.** If you're on schedule fine, but if you are behind, work with the person by offering your assistance. Train him early and continue his training throughout the activity as appropriate.

  — **Demand results, but do not expect perfection.** If the activity is on target to be successful, do not allow minor mistakes or different methods to upset you.

  — **Encourage their independence.** Let them do it their way. Do not always change their decision and look over their shoulder.

  — **Do not allow differences of opinion to interfere with the success of the activity.** Remember, the results are more important than the methods utilized.

  — **DO NOT relieve them of their responsibility too early.** This is a judgment, but if you do relieve them of their job, it will shake their confidence and most likely end any possibility that they will participate in future activities.

— **REWARD THEIR PERFORMANCE.** As we discussed in the awards and incentives area, people crave recognition. Your recognition of their successful accomplishments will motivate them and other members and them to further participation in the organization.

SUMMARY

Delegating responsibility is not a sign of weakness. An effective delegator (leader) is a team player who is more concerned with the success of the team than he is with his personal success. He knows that when the team wins, he wins and that there is enough glory for everyone on the team. He is usually highly respected by his team and has little problem recruiting people to delegate responsibilities to because his members know that they are a respected and valuable contributor to the team.

RECRUITING ACTIVITY CHAIRMEN

Importance

The future of any organization requires the continual recruitment of new members, activity chairmen and board members. Board members should **NEVER** chair activities as it will be detrimental to the long range success of your organization.

How To Find A Chairman

- ASK YOUR FRIENDS (IF THEY'RE NOT A MEMBER ASK THEM TO JOIN!)
- AT MEETINGS
  - Look for the gleam in the eye of a new member at the meeting.
  - Always approach them one-on-one.
  - Ask them what their interests are.
  - If they are not interested in your activity refer them to another officer.
  - DO NOT ask for a chairman in front of the entire membership.
  - Make the opportunity important to them.
  - If they will not accept, ask them to be a sub-chairman. This makes recruiting a chairman easier if you already have several committee volunteers.
- AT ACTIVITIES
  - Sub-Chairmen are excellent prospects if they have been managed properly.
  - Make them aware of their opportunity to be a star.

Important Points To Remember !

- DO NOT hesitate to ask for help from a more experienced officer if you are having a hard time finding a chairman.
- The board should not allow any member to become involved in too many activities as you might allow that member to become a victim of burnout.

MANAGING NON-PERFORMERS

This is the part of managing a business or volunteer organization that makes a manager pull his hair out. Why can't everyone be as motivated to do as good a job as you are? Non-performing people are a fact of life and come with a position of leadership. There are many reasons that a person may not perform. He may have burned out (lost his motivation), be in an improper position, be temporarily overloaded with responsibilities, etc. Sometimes he is looking for a way out of his responsibility without embarrassing himself.

The better you manage the non-performing person, the more successful a term you will have as an organization leader.

Before you can motivate a non-performer you must first identify the problem and arrive at an acceptable solution.

Identify The Problem

When you work to identify the problem, make sure that you find the problem and not a symptom. Sometimes this requires more work, but as in medicine, if you solve a symptom the problem will keep reoccurring until you solve it or the patient dies (leaves the organization).

Before you criticize the non-performer, review the following check-list to make sure that you are providing effective leadership. You will notice that these items were also discussed in the delegation area.

- **I know him as a person.**
  People will perform for close personal friends first. If you do not know him well he will not feel any responsibility to you as a friend.

- **I have been fair and honest with him.**
  Do not allow organization politics to cost you an effective volunteer.

- **I have encouraged him and supported his efforts.**
  Words of thank you and thank you notes let people know that you are aware of their efforts.

- **I detailed his responsibilities.**
  A written job description is best, but a one-on-one visit will also work.

- **I told him what the organization expected of him.**
- **I told him how his contribution would enhance the efforts of the whole organization.**
  This will make the volunteer feel more responsible and and obtain a broader perspective of the activity.
- **I assisted him in establishing his goals.**
  Do not do this for him. He may set higher goals than you would.
- **I provided initial and on-going training.**
  This will not only help him to execute his job, but prepare him for a leadership role in the organization.
- **I described the opportunities he could have from being successful.**
  Based on his abilities and ambition, a well placed word from a respected leader can motivate a volunteer to hold positions that he may not have ever dreamed about.
  As a director in a Jaycee chapter, a past president told me that he would kick my tail if I did not run for president 2 years from then. I had never thought about running for president, but the confidence that leader showed in me made me think and motivated me to set and achieve that goal.
  This is your opportunity to change peoples lives and improve your organization.
- **I did not circumvent his authority or constantly look over his shoulder.**
  He has to feel that when you delegated the job to him that you delegated the authority along with the responsibility.
- **I recognized his successes with rewards and corrected his shortcomings in private.**
  Remember to praise in public and reprimand in private. If you embarrass him, he will not feel any obligation to help you make your goals.

It is important as a leader that you answer yes to each of these statements. If you can not, the problem may be in your leadership. If it is, you need to begin immediately to correct your performance. No leader is perfect, and one who is afraid of admitting an error and the need for continued personal improvement will speak to deaf ears when they try to correct their members performance.

If you are correctly performing the above functions, then it is time to look at the non-performer.

- **Has he overcommitted to the organization?**
  This is something the leadership of the organization should prevent. Often a person will not realize how much time a job will take or can not say no when asked to help. The leadership of the organization can see more than the person and should not allow this to happen.

- **Is he having problems at home or at work?**
  You may have to really probe to find out this information. People naturally do not want others to know about their problems.

- **Ask him if he understands his job.**
  Just because you explained the job to him does not mean that he understood what you said. Asking him if he understood is the only way you will know for sure.

- **Is he afraid to ask for help?**
  It is amazing how often people struggle with a responsibility but will not ask for help. He feels that asking for help is a sign of weakness. In business this fear extends to being afraid that he may lose his job or a pay raise. In volunteer work, he fears that people will lose respect for him or her will not be recognized for his contributions when the job is over.

Alternative Solutions

Once you have determined the problem, it is time to examine the alternatives available to correct the situation.

- **Additional Training.** This may be one-on-one or part of a group session. It should be based on the needs of the individual.
- **Praise And Encourage Them.** Sometimes a public display of praise or a thank you note is all that is needed.
- **Re-assign A Portion Of His Responsibility.** If he is overloaded, assign part of his duties to another person.
- **Spend Time With Him To Help In Over-Coming The Problems.**
  Personal attention not only shows him that you care, but gives you the opportunity to provide additional motivation

and training. Do not talk too much. Let him talk, as you learn more by listening than by talking.

- **Reassign Them To Another Supervisor.** If a personality conflict arises, this can correct it.
- **Utilize New Management Techniques When Working With Them.** You may have to begin meeting him in person regularly, setting up phone appointments, etc., which he will find more acceptable than your current techniques.
- **Give Him A New Job Assignment.** His interest and abilities may dictate that you move him to another position. Think of yourself as a baseball manager.
- **If You Are The Problem—Straighten Your Self Out.**
- **Last Resort—Replace Him.**
  No one likes to fire someone, but if the previous steps do not work, it may be necessary. Give him a 30-90 day period to correct his performance. Give him a specific list of responsibilities, a time deadline and monitor him daily. He will usually either perform or will look for ways to resign.

If you must replace someone, do it in person and treat him like you would like to be treated. Remember that this is a volunteer environment and you do not want to hurt the individual as it may rebound and hurt the organization or you.

INTERNAL POLITICS

Internal politics can be the invisible enemy of progress toward organizational goals because of the energies expended by one person or a group against another person or group to benefit himself or his group rather than the organization as a whole.

The factionalism that results from internal politics is one of the greatest problems that an organization faces. No organization, volunteer or otherwise, is immune from the subversion of its goals by individuals or groups who are only interested in their own goals.

Recognizing and managing these individuals or groups is a tremendous challenge, but essential in order to achieve the goals of the organization.

Signs that will expose that the true motivation of an individual is for his own goals instead of the organization goals include:

- The first thought considered in any matter is how it will benefit him and not the organization.
- If it is not his idea, then he is not interested in contributing.
- He will not accept or volunteer for any job which has little or no public recognition.
- He is always jealous of the success and accomplishments of others.
- If he can not achieve a desired objective, then he will make sure that no one else does either.
- He lives by the motto of "Don't get mad, get even!"
- He worries about who to blame for the failure of an event and expends efforts to protect himself instead of spending all of his efforts to insure that the event is successful.
- He reads the popular opinion of others before deciding what action to take. This leads to an inconsistency of action instead of action based on principle. Thomas Jefferson said: "In matters of principle, stand like a rock. In matters of taste, swim with the current."
- He makes deals on who or what he will vote for based on your voting for his activity or candidate.

How do we recognize and manage individuals who display the signs discussed above?

First, practicing the six steps to building a successful team that are discussed in the personnel management section will help you to establish common organizational goals and work effectively toward their achievement.

Second, review your awards and incentives program. There should be a purpose for each award. Some individuals will try to win an award without accomplishing its requirements. If members of the organization feel an undeserving person won an award because he circumvented the rules or had influence with the person or group who decided the recipient, they will be more difficult to motivate by the opportunity of being recognized with an award. This itself will reduce the accomplishments of an organization.

Third, test the true motivation of the aggressive or hard charging individual. Offer him an opportunity that has little or no public exposure, but one that benefits the organization. If he accepts, you know that you have a team player who is only concerned with the accomplishment of the organization's goals. If he declines, he might be primarily interested in his own goals and should be managed carefully to insure that he positively contributes to the organization.

Conclusion

Most members of an organization can spot an individual who only is concerned with himself. They will not want to help that person to achieve his selfish goals, but they will eagerly assist someone who selflessly gives of himself to a cause that is also important to them.

It is ironic, but you can not give more to an organization than you receive. It doesn't matter how hard you try or how selfless you are, this is true. The benefits may not be short term, and they may not be visible, but they will occur in the form of personal growth and opportunities that would not have otherwise occurred. This will provide an individual more success than if he spent all of his efforts trying to achieve his goals by himself.

FILLING BOARD VACANCIES—PLANNED TURNOVER ?

Turnover of board members during a year is inevitable. This can be a traumatic experience or one that you and your entire board can perceive as a positive experience.

Planning for turnover can be one of the most important areas that you as a president must address. The following ideas are worth remembering when planning and managing your board.

- **Turnover is inevitable**

  If you recognize this, anticipate and plan for it, and you will be more successful.

- **Turnover can be positive**

  Some of the turnover on a board are people who have not performed. This allows you to replace them with people you know will perform.

- **Personnel Pool**

  Always, always have a list of people who are good director and officer candidates. Break your list in areas of responsibility by board position.

- **Take your candidate's strengths into consideration**

  Look at the strengths and goals of your candidates. If you help them achieve their goals, they will help you achieve your goals. Everyone is not a good candidate for every office.

- **You do not always have to bring a new person onto your board**

  Sometimes you may want to move a person from one director spot to another one. Beware, this can cause problems in two areas instead of one.

- **You do not have to fill an opening immediately**

  Filling an open position with the wrong person is worse than having it vacant. Make someone a standing chairman first, or leave the spot open as an incentive for the people who want it for a period of time. Make sure you fill it with the best possible person!

- **Your organization's annual plan is your best indicator of upcoming board turnover**

  If a board member is not achieving the goals as they were planned you better prepare for turnover. Work with the person first to avoid his resignation or firing, but his incompletion of short term goals is a telltale sign.

- **Involve your executive board in the process**
  Have your executive board maintain its own personnel pool to make recommendations to you. This will train the board members for future leadership, and earn you support from them for the candidates you recommend to the board for approval.

Just remember that all it takes to create a board vacancy is a car accident, job transfer or illness. **Proper Prior Planning Prevents Pitifully Poor Performances.** Will you be ready for your next board vacancy?

FACING ADVERSITY

Adversity is inevitable during the year. The way you and your board handle it will determine your success or failure.

Planning, in detail, for every potential problem and establishing contingency plans will minimize the number of crises you will experience.

Perseverance to your year long goal is imperative! You must not let short term problems sway your course. The president must maintain a positive outlook on the long term and turn every negative event into a positive opportunity.

A joke in my Jaycee chapter stated that the outgoing president would present the incoming president three envelopes. They would tell the new president to open an envelope when adversity struck and the envelope would contain advice that would overcome the adversity. When the first adversity arrived, the president opened the first envelope and it said, "Blame it on the past president." The president stood up at the next meeting and blamed everything on the past president. Everything became smooth until a few months later when a second adversity struck. The president opened the second envelope and it said, "Blame it on the national organization." At the next meeting the president did just that and the adversity went away. Toward the end of the year a third adversity struck. The president opened the third envelope and it said, "Prepare three envelopes!"

All things normal, you will experience a slump during the year. It may occur in the summer, Christmas holidays or another time. If you wait until it occurs to recognize and manage it you will be too late. To minimize a slump, forecast slumps and plan activities to offset their effect.

Admiral "Bull" Halsey of World War II fame once said, "There are no great men, only good men who overcome great challenges." Adversity affects people in different ways:

- People who talk big in an organization are always the first to disappear when adversity strikes. Beware of these people.
- Adversity brings out a person's true character. Anyone can do an easy or fun job, but the people who do the tough jobs that others shy away from are people with special character.
- Adversity breeds success. No great idea occurs without

solving an existing adversity.

- Adversity is inevitable, if you expect it, look for the positives in it and make decisions to keep your organization on track for your year long goal, you will be successful.

AVOIDING BURNOUT

Burnout occurs when a volunteer reaches a point where he is no longer interested in participating in an organization or event.

Burnout is one of the largest problems in a volunteer organization.

Causes for burnout vary. One of the most prevalent reasons is that the volunteer wants to do a great job, but is afraid to ask others for help. Burnout results from the self-imposed pressure of attempting to do everything by oneself.

Burnout can not be totally eliminated, but is minimized by:
- Good planning
- Good training
- Delegating responsibilities
- Always have your next goal in mind before you accomplish your current goal. This will prevent you from reaching the mindset that you've accomplished everything you wanted to accomplish.

EXECUTIVE COMMITTEE

As in businesses, the establishment of an executive committee offers a volunteer organization several benefits.

- **Saves Time**
  - By meeting before the board meetings to establish the agenda and reviewing business that the board will discuss.
  - By authorizing certain decisions to be made by the executive committee instead of the full board.

- **Anticipate Controversy**
  To inform the president of all business to be discussed and the committee's opinion on these issues. One of the worst things that can happen to the president at a board meeting is to have a controversial item of business brought up without his knowledge.

- **Quicker Decisions**
  The executive committee can be quickly polled by telephone to make a decision in a crisis situation.

- **Better Management**
  The executive committee offers the organization an additional opportunity to monitor its plan and activities.

- **Additional Motivation**
  Provides the president an opportunity to motivate and inspire the executive committee to greater performance.

The executive committee normally consists of the president, all vice-presidents, the secretary and treasurer. Other individuals may be included based on the needs of your organization.

BOARD OF DIRECTORS

Once you have trained your board and have written your annual plan of action, it is time to execute the plan.

Managing your board of directors to successfully execute their responsibilities can be frustrating and/or rewarding depending on your management skills.

As we have discussed previously, each board member is different, which requires you to use different methods of motivation and discipline. We have also stated that if a person does not achieve his intermediate goals, he will be unlikely to achieve his annual goals. As his leader, you are responsible for monitoring his progress and insuring his success.

Two tools can assist you in managing your board:

- **Gantt Chart**—We discussed establishing the gantt chart in the planning section. We will now look at using it to make your job of supervising your board members more efficient. Gantt charts show each activity and the critical dates and tasks to be accomplished by that date. These will be listed on one page for each board member so he can see his major milestone dates for the year at a quick glance.

  Once you have filled in the chart by the responsibilities of each board member, organize the pages by officer with each officer's board members behind the officer's name.

  The president should review weekly with each officer the progress of his directors. The officers should also review weekly the progress of each of their directors. If you find that you are behind on an activity, you can take appropriate actions to bring the activity back on schedule. This will eliminate the possibility of falling behind on an activity more than one week, help avoid crises situations and make your leadership of the organization more enjoyable.

- **Checklist**—When you contact your officers and directors for their weekly progress report, a gantt chart may not include all the things that you wish to discuss with the board member.

I suggest that you keep a folder for each board member. During the week, make notes about the upcoming progress report. Include the critical dates from the gantt chart, additional details for those activities and any other business you would like to discuss.

A face-to-face meeting is better than discussing these items on the telephone. The meeting may be held at breakfast, lunch, dinner, after work, etc., but scheduling it at the same time every week will simplify your schedules and help insure that you will do it.

The president must think ahead of his officers and have items on the checklist that the officers may not have planned for at that date. The officers must think ahead of their directors. The officers will probably add items to their checklist after meeting with the president.

When you review the checklist with the appropriate officer or director make notes concerning the status or progress of each item. If an item has not been completed obtain a firm written commitment of the date it will be completed. Put any items that are not completed at the top of the checklist the next week, and do not remove them until they are completed. That will let the board member know that you are not going to forget the responsibility and that he should complete it if he does not want you asking him about it weekly.

The checklist is an excellent tool to use with non-performers. It can help turnaround a person's performance or be the justification for his dismissal.

Maintaining all the checklists in their folders for the year provides you a chronology of the activities in each area. This information can benefit the next person to hold the position and help in preparing your annual report of the progress of the organization.

EFFECTIVE BOARD MEETINGS

The purpose of board meetings is to monitor current activities, evaluate progress toward your annual goal, approve new actvities, motivate your board to achieve more and discuss other business. All of this is designed for you to keep the group headed toward your goal.

Similar to membership meetings rules:

- Prepare a written agenda.
- Start the meeting on time.
- Allocate time on the agenda for discussing each item of business.
- End the meeting on time. If you end the meeting early you will be a hero, but if the meeting ends late everyone will leave the meeting on a negative note.

Using Parliamentary Procedure

The use of parliamentary procedure sets the stage for conducting a timely and professional board meeting.

As president, it is better to start your term being too strict about parliamentary procedure and easing up later in the year than it is starting too relaxed and trying to increase discipline. It is similar to the military. Boot camp has the most discipline and the least amount of freedom. After the troops are trained about military procedures and complete boot camp, they are given more freedom and a little less discipline. Show your board early your leadership style and that you are serious about discharging your responsibilities to successfully lead the organization. As they blend into a team and are trained on the operation of the board, they will become more efficient. When they become more efficient and respect your leadership, you will be able to allow a lighthearted moment in a board meeting without losing the respect of your board members. If you are perceived early in your term as not being serious about your responsibilities, you will never be able to get your board members to be serious about their responsibilities.

As president and leader of the meeting, do not take sides on an issue while you are presiding. If you do this you will lose the respect of your board. If you want to discuss an issue, pass the gavel to the next officer in command. An alert president will know how each of the officers feels about an issue. This will allow them to plan when to pass the gavel to speak during a discussion so an officer taking the other side of an issue will not hold the gavel and its power.

Do not be afraid to use the gavel to call someone "out of order" if their discussion is not germane to the business at hand. Your board will respect you for respecting their time.

Keep a one page summary of the types of motions and their rules by the lectern, but do not let anyone know that you have it. The president should know more about parliamentary procedure than anyone on the board. When a controversial discussion occurs, your knowledge of the rules will help you to maintain order in the meeting.

Obtain a copy of *Roberts Rules of Order* to assist you with specific rules and for a reference as questions arise.

Executive Session

At the end of each board meeting, conduct an executive session. Ask all guests at the meeting to leave. The business discussed is confidential and the board should be advised of this fact. You may want to limit the types of topics to be discussed during the executive session in your by-laws or leave it to the discretion of each year's board.

Joint Board Meetings

During the transition between the current administration and the upcoming administration, consider conducting a joint board meeting. This will serve as a training tool for the incoming board. Have each director report the activities of his responsibility during the year. The current president can also pass the gavel at this meeting, which will signify the passing of the power and responsibility for the organization.

Past President Attending Board Meetings

If your past president is a member of your board, it is advisable that he does not attend the first few meetings of a new administration. This will allow him time to relax after his term. It will also permit the new president to establish his own leadership of the board and the organization.

Summary

Your board members are the leaders of the organization. Your job is to lead and manage them and their job is to manage the membership.

The board meeting is a very important forum for exercising your leadership. Properly conducted board meetings are imperative for you to build a unified team and have a successful term of office.

EFFECTIVE MEMBERSHIP MEETINGS

There are four steps to having effective membership meetings:

PLANNING

I. **Location**

- Parking—Make sure that the location has sufficient, easy to find parking.

- Geographic Location—Seek a location that is centrally located to the majority of your members.

- Room—Hold your meetings in the same location if possible. Making it easier to find the meeting will increase your attendance.

  — Size—A room that looks full is better than a room that looks empty. Set up fewer chairs than you need.
  You can always add more chairs.
  — Lighting—Make sure that it will suit your purpose.
  — Sound System—Test the system when you evaluate a possible location.
  — Lectern and Head Table Set-up—Locate the head table in an area of the room that will allow the majority of the people attending the meeting to see and hear the program.
  — Meals—All food items need to be served quickly without disturbing the program. A buffet is an ideal way to have your meals, if you have a large enough group. Avoid making a guarantee of the number of meals that the group will order. This exposes you to a financial risk.
  — Bar—Do not allow a bar to be open too long as it may lead to potentially embarrassing situations. Close the bar during the formal meeting to eliminate additional distractions and alcohol related problems.

- Double check with the manager before every meeting. Confirm the room, etc. It is amazing how often a misunderstanding occurs between a group and a location for a meeting.

- Always arrive at the location early to make sure the room is set-up and everything is ready.

II. **Program**

A speaker or outside program can be informative and a drawing card to attract members, guests and the media to your meetings. Controversial and/or current event topics breed interest, which will increase your attendance also.

- Speaker—Inviting a speaker from the outside requires you to communicate before, during and after the meeting to the speaker.
  - Send the speaker a written invitation.
  - After the speaker has accepted, send a written confirmation. Include:
    - The date of the meeting.
    - The location with a map.
    - The length of time he will have to speak.
    - Ask him not to make a sales pitch.
    - Suggest a topic or information that the membership would like to learn about.
    - Send him information about your organization so he can anticipate the type of group that he will address. This will influence his speech preparation.
    - Advise him about any expenses that the group will pay.
    - Request an introduction to use during the meeting.
    - Let him know if his spouse is invited and how those expenses will be handled.
    - Tell him who his "host" will be. The "host" is the person who will greet the speaker upon arrival or pick him up at the airport, and remain with him during his visit to make his visit a pleasant experience.
    - Advise him of the seating arrangement in the room. This is a simple courtesy that will make him feel more comfortable when he arrives.
  - Confirm that the speaker will attend before the meeting.
  - At the meeting, advise the speaker again about the length of his speech. Set up a signal that you will give him when his time is up. If he will not sit down, stand up interrupt the conversation at a convenient time to end his presentation.

Using the "hook" is important because you **can not** let a long winded speaker ruin your meeting.

— Give the speaker a gift for sharing their time with you. This may be a gift certificate, donated meal for two, etc.

— Send the speaker a **personal thank you** note the next day in addition to a formal thank you from the organization. This is not only polite, but also impressive.

- Business—If you are a relatively small group, you may conduct your business at your membership meetings. If you are larger, it is advisable to conduct all business at your board meetings. Conducting business with a large group makes it difficult to adhere to your agenda and produces long meetings, which no one likes.

- Awards—Make sure all awards are ready. (Follow the awards information previously discussed in this section).

III. **Administration**

- Have a printed agenda with times on it.

    Example

6:00 p.m.	**Call to Order**
6:01 p.m.	**Invocation**
6:02 p.m.	**Pledge of Allegiance**
6:03 p.m.	**Introduction of Guests**
6:08 p.m.	**Member Introductions**
6:13 p.m.	**Activity Announcements**
6:25 p.m.	**Awards**
6:35 p.m.	**Speaker or Program**
6:55 p.m.	**Closing Announcements**
7:00 p.m.	**Adjourn**

- Have name tags available. Have "guest" on the guest name tags so that members can introduce themselves and make them feel welcome.

- Have a guest and a member sign-in sheet. This provides you a list of potential new members and informs you who is and is not attending your meetings.

- The board is responsible for establishing the number of meetings per month and types as a matter of policy.

- The President sets the precedent for the dress code at the meetings. If the president dresses in business attire (i.e. a suit or dress) other members will dress accordingly. The president should ask the board to follow his lead. This will reinforce the dress code.

- Attendance—Each organization must decide whether meeting attendance is required, and the number of acceptable absences.
- Make sure the directors know their responsibilities at the meetings.
- Have someone responsible for bringing all flags and banners.
- Have contingency plans prepared in the event your original plans fail. Alternatives for the location, speaker, equipment and date should be prepared.

PROMOTION

- Mail the agenda to the members before the meeting.
- Publish the meeting in any organization publication.
- Have a phone bank to call members to invite them to the meeting.
- Send VIP's special invitations to the meeting.
- Notify newspapers, radio stations and community access television stations and ask that they announce the meeting as a public service announcement.
- Offer incentives to increase meeting attendance. One example is to have every member in the organization's name in a hat at the sign-in table. At the end of the meeting draw a name. The winner will win one half of the pot (usually $5, with $5 added every meeting that there is no winner) if they are at the meeting. Draw a name of an attending member. If the winning member shook hands with the other member before the meeting they win the other half of the pot. As the pot rises, members will attend to try to win it. This also encourages your members to meet and visit with each other at the meeting.

CONDUCTING THE MEETING

- Have a designated greeter at the door to make everyone feel welcome.
- **START ON TIME**—If you start the meeting on time, members will learn that the meetings will start on time and

start arriving early. This respects their time!
- Introduce the guests. Have the person who brought the guest make the introduction. Applaud the guest for attending and thank the member for bringing a prospective member.
- Maximize participation in the meeting by giving as many different people the opportunity to speak.
- Allow social time before or after the meeting.
- Make anyone who would like to make an announcement request permission. This eliminates wasted time and surprise announcements that you do not want.
- Close the bar during the meeting.
- Make the awards presentation EXCITING!
- Have water to drink and place cards at the head table.
- BE ENTHUSIASTIC! This will excite others about being involved in the organization.
- **FINISH THE MEETING ON TIME.** People will not continue to attend meetings that are too long and start to drag. Again, this shows the membership that you respect their time and other commitments.

POST MEETING EVALUATION
- Send thank you notes to all appropriate people.
- Publish a press release if appropriate to the meeting.
- Prepare the minutes of the meeting.
- Evaluate the meeting.
- Gather opinions of the meeting.

These guidelines will produce successful meetings, which will enhance your organization's efforts to achieve your goals.

MEETING CHECKLIST

PLANNING

_____ LOCATION CONFIRMED

_____ CONFIRM SPEAKER, OBTAIN GIFT

_____ PRINT AGENDA

_____ NAME TAGS

_____ SIGN-IN SHEET

_____ CONTINGENCY PLAN (SPEAKER, LOCATION AND EQUIPMENT)

_____ FLAGS AND BANNER(S)

_____ BOARD KNOWS ITS RESPONSIBILITIES

_____ PREPARE AWARDS

PROMOTION

_____ MAIL AGENDA

_____ NOTIFY VIP'S

_____ SEND PRESS RELEASES

_____ MEETING INFORMATION IN ORGANIZATION'S PUBLICATION(S)

_____ PHONE BANK

CONDUCTING THE MEETING

_____ ARRIVE EARLY

_____ CHECK THE FACILITY AND EQUIPMENT

_____ SELECT A GREETER

_____ START ON TIME

_____ APPROVE AND ARRANGE ACTIVITY ANNOUNCEMENTS

_____ HEAD TABLE

_____ END ON TIME

POST MEETING EVALUATION

_____ SEND THANK YOU'S

_____ PRESS RELEASE

_____ TYPE MINUTES

_____ EVALUATE THE MEETING

_____ ASK OTHERS THEIR OPINION ON THE MEETING

ORGANIZATION FINANCES

"A trustee is held to something stricter than the morals of the market-place. Not honesty alone, but the punctilio of an honor the most sensitive, is the standard of behavior."

Benjamin N. Carduzo (1870-1938)

ORGANIZATION FINANCES

Inefficient management of the organization's finances is a cause of internal problems. Treat your organization like a business. To do that you must exercise professional financial management techniques, have an effective fundraising program and control expenses. In this section, we will examine ideas that will help you to improve the financial management of your organization.

INCORPORATION

As we discussed in the legal counsel section of the administrative area, incorporating your organization is one of your first priorities. The most important reason is to limit the personal liability of your board members against financial loss or lawsuit. It also is a prerequisite for obtaining a tax exempt and/or charitable organization (501c3) status.

As a part of incorporating, file your organization's name, trademark, logo, slogan, etc. with the Secretary of State or appropriate office in your state for trademark and copyright protection. This will protect you from having unauthorized people use them in a manner that would do harm to your organization's finance or reputation.

Maintain proper records on the regulations governing your trademark or copyright names. If members in the future are unaware of their expiration, you may lose the right to use the name and all of the efforts your group has exercised to establish the credibility of that name to someone else. Regulations in your area may or may not require an annual or periodic fee to maintain your trademark, copyright or corporate charter. Check with the Secretary of State's office in your state regarding regulations that will apply to you.

TAX EXEMPT STATUS AND
CHARITABLE FOUNDATIONS

As a non-profit organization you certainly want to obtain status as a tax exempt organization and may want to establish a foundation so you can obtain a 501c3 designation and be able to solicit tax deductible charitable contributions.

These are two different designations. Seek the advice of an attorney (who is hopefully the organization's legal counsel) when you apply for either tax exempt or 501c3 status.

Let's explore both individually and how an organization might benefit from them.

Tax Exempt Status

After you have incorporated, submit Form 1023 to the Internal Revenue Service (IRS) requesting a tax exemption for your organization. IRS publication 557, "Tax Exempt Status For Your Organization," can provide you assistance with your application. Submit the comparable form to your state agency to obtain tax exemption in your state.

Receiving your tax exempt status does not mean that you will not pay any taxes. You still may be liable for some business or property taxes. You will be exempt from income taxes and will receive a number, which will exempt you from paying local sales taxes. Instruct your members of this fact so they will not needlessly pay sales tax on items the organization purchases.

Two important reports must be filed regularly to maintain your tax exempt status. First, you must file your tax return and not show a profit. If you have a surplus of income at year end, expend it according to your annual plan so that you finish the year with zero net income. Second, pay the appropriate withholding taxes for your employees. If you do not do this, you may not only lose your tax exempt status, but be put out of operation as well.

501c3 Charitable Status

This status offers an organization and its donors the most favorable tax benefits and it is much more difficult to obtain than a tax exempt status.

A 501c3 organization can be private or public, is non-profitable and has already received a tax exemption. It must be incorporated exclusively for its stated charitable purpose, which means you will need to establish a separate corporation for your charitable activities. The purpose of the corporation is usually to benefit educational, religious, charitable or scientific organizations or individuals.

501c3 status offers several benefits. Because donors to the organization receive tax deductions, it is easier to solicit donations. You may also qualify for matching donations from a person's employer. Charitable groups qualify for a special bulk mail rate from the postal service. Another benefit can be that you will qualify for discounts on items you purchase. And finally, it can allow you to acquire and hold land and buildings to conduct the organization's business.

The following steps must be completed in order to obtain 501c3 status:

- Establish a foundation.
- Set up a separate corporation. A separate board of directors will be necessary. You may want to establish your group's board members as the members of the charitable group and elect the board from them. The government regulations are much tighter on the use of funds of a charitable group. Your corporate purpose should be to donate the funds to your organization for its charitable activities or to other qualifying organizations or individuals.
- Establish a constitution and by-laws.
- Submit a form SS-4 to the IRS to obtain a federal employer identification number. This needs to be done even if you do not currently have any employees.
- Submit form 1023 to the IRS requesting a tax exemption.
- Submit the appropriate form to your state government requesting a tax exemption.
- Apply to the postmaster for a special bulk mailing permit.

It normally takes a few months to obtain all the necessary approvals. Do not be surprised or alarmed if you are asked for more information concerning your application. This is a sought after designation and the government does a good job to prevent groups from abusing its privileges.

LEGAL

Two areas that are important to the financial stability of the organization and that have legal implications are insurance and bonding.

Insurance

Insuring your organization's, members, property and activities will eliminate the possibility of the organization being financially ruined by one unusual incident.

Establish an insurance committee who will research your current insurance coverage and future needs. Review your entire program annually.

A comprehensive liability policy will cover the majority of areas where you may be exposed. Special policies or riders are needed for:

- **Product Liability**—If you serve food or beverages this will protect you against a lawsuit for food poisoning or a product problem.
- **Equipment**—If you have a computer or other equipment, they may not be covered by your comprehensive policy and may require a rider or a special policy.
- **Real Property**—If you own a building, you will need insurance to cover it against loss from a fire, flood, etc.
- **Special Events**—This may include rain insurance for an outside activity or even insurance for a hole-in-one contest at a golf tournament.
- **Alcohol Sales**—You may need to have special coverage for serving or selling alcohol. This is an area that is changing very quickly because of dram shop laws that hold people who serve alcohol liable if someone they served causes an accident. Consult with your insurance representative on this area because of variations in local laws.

Bonding

A bond is similar to an insurance policy. You pay a premium for a policy that protects the organization from a covered person misusing organization funds.

Normally, coverage is provided for all paid staff people and all officers who sign on bank accounts or cash authorize the expenditure of funds. Your legal counsel and insurance representatives are the best sources to consult in establishing this coverage.

If you have a frequent turnover of people, you may want to bond a position rather than a person. This will cover you regardless of who occupies the covered position and requires less changes in the policy as different people assume the covered positions.

FINANCIAL MANAGEMENT

In this area, I will discuss financial statements, accounts payable, and general rules for the use of bank accounts.

There are four financial statements that we will discuss. They are your annual budget, balance sheet, income statement and cash flow analysis.

Annual Budget

As we discussed in the planning section, your annual budget is a by-product of your annual planning retreat. It lists a budgeted amount of net income or deficit for every activity, event or program that you conduct. It also lists all administrative salaries and expenses, such as office mortgage, utilities, postage, etc.

Have all expenses exceeding a budgeted amount approved by your board of directors before they are expended.

Your ability to meet your financial goals for the year will depend on how well you use your budget as an ongoing management tool. You will be much more successful if you strictly adhere to it than if you ignore it.

Income Statement

The income statement is designed to state any income or loss for a period and year to date.

It enables you to monitor your budget for any given period and the year for each line item. Surplus and deficiencies will be denoted for each line item, which will help you in managing your budget.

Two examples of how you might organize your income statement are shown on the next page.

I. Combined Income and Expense Statement (shows year to date)
Income Statement Thru 6/30/8x

Item	Approved Bud	Inc.	Exp.	Net Dif.	Variation to Bud.
Corp Sponsor	$5,000	$3,000	$ 500	$2,500	($2,500)
Postage	$ 250	-0-	$ 100	$ 150	($ 100)
TOTAL	$5,250	$3,000	$ 600	$2,650	$2,600

II. Separate Income and Expense Statement (also separates month and year to date).
Income Statement Thru 6/30/8x

Description	Annual Budget	Current Month			Year to Date		
		Budget	Actual	Var.	Budget	Actual	Var.
Income							
Corp Sponsor	$5,000	$ 416	$ 300	-$ 116	$2500	$2000	-$ 500
Fundraising	$2,400	$ 200	$ 255	$ 55	$1200	$1550	$ 350
Total Income	$7,400	$ 616	$ 555	-$ 61	$3700	$3550	-$ 150
Expenses							
Postage	$ 250	$ 21	$ 15	$ 6	$ 125	$ 150	-$ 25
Payroll	$4,800	$ 400	$ 400	-0-	$2400	$2300	$ 100
Total Expenses	$5,050	$ 421	$ 415	$ 6	$2525	$2450	$ 75
Surplus or Deficit Income	$2,350	$ 195	$ 140	-$ 55	$1175	$1100	-$ 75

Balance Sheet

The balance sheet lists the assets and liabilities of the organization. The difference in assets and liabilities determines the net worth or deficit.

Assets include cash on hand or in the bank, accounts receivable less an estimate for uncollectable amounts, real property and inventory or personal property.

Liabilities include accounts payable, notes payable, long term debt, deferred income, fund balance and payroll taxes.

An example of a balance sheet might be:

Assets

Cash on hand	$ 100.00
Bank Account #1	1,000.00
Accounts Receivable	300.00
Less allowance	(100.00)
Inventory	500.00
Real Property	20,000.00
Less depreciation	(5,000.00)
Personal Property	2,500.00
TOTAL ASSETS	$19,300.00

Liabilities

Accounts payable	200.00
Payroll taxes and withholding payable	1,000.00
Deferred Income	-0-
Long Term Debt	10,000.00
Short Term Notes Payable	1,500.00
SUB-TOTAL LIABILITIES	$12,700.00
NET WORTH	$ 6,600.00
TOTAL LIABILITIES	$19,300.00

Cash Flow

Just because your organization generates sufficient revenue, does not mean that you will not experience cash flow problems where expenses occur faster than income.

An on-going cash flow analysis will help you to forecast periods of excesses and shortages of cash. This will also help you to plan times of the year when you need to devote more efforts to generate revenue.

To analyze cash flow, construct a chart (see example below) that has column headings across the page by month and a total column at the end of the page. Down the left side of the page, divide the page into rows for beginning cash balance, income by category, total income, expenses by category, total expenses and the month ending surplus or deficit.

	Ja	Fe	Ma	Ap	Ma	Ju	Jl	Au	Se	Oc	No	De	Tot
	(ONE MONTH EXAMPLE)												
Beg. Bal	$ 500												
INCOME													
Dues	50												
Interest	5												
Activity 1	250												
Activity 2	$ 125												
Total	$ 930												
EXPENSES													
Office	300												
Staff	400												
Activity 1	100												
Activity 2	20												
Total	$ 820												
End Cash Bal	$ 110												

A cash flow statement is created by completing the chart with figures from your annual budget and previous experience. Monthly as the year progresses replace your budgeted figures with actual figures and project the remainder of the year.

If a deficit appears for any month or the year, you will have to raise income and cut or delay expenses by priority during that period. If you project a surplus for the year, prioritize uses for the money. A non-profit corporation is not allowed to make a profit so be prepared in case you are fortunate and this happens.

A properly managed cash flow statement will not only improve your organization's financial management, but will also transcend into a more efficient operation in the non-financial areas as well.

Accounts Payable

Like a business, effectively processing your accounts payable requires a few basic guidelines. Implementing these will make your organization more efficient and will result in a better working relationship with the people who extended purchasing terms to you.

First, utilize a check request form that has to be approved by the activity chairman and supervising board member before it is submitted to the treasurer for payment. Include a space for the line of your annual budget that will be debited by the payment. Have the treasurer sign the form after he makes sure the expense does not exceed the amount of the line item in the annual budget or each line item in the activity budget. Paying careful attention to these details will save you money and minimize miscommunications about the expenses you will pay.

Second, pay all bills within 30 days. Failure to do this may cost you the opportunity to receive these favorable terms from this vendor in the future. If you have a computer, schedule your payments weekly, if possible, toward the end of the 30 day period to maximize your cash flow and earn additional interest from the money in your bank account.

Third, establish a limit in your by-laws, which allows the president to authorize expending an amount of funds without board approval. A sum of $ 100 to $ 500 is customary based on the size of your budget. This will save time in an emergency because the president will not have to call a special board meeting to approve the expenditure. You may also want to set a slightly higher limit that the executive board can approve. An acceptable figure may be $250 to $1,000. Any amounts over these limits need to be approved by the board of directors prior to their expenditure.

Bank Accounts

To minimize the possibility of accidental or intentional problems with your bank accounts:

- **Establish as few accounts as possible.**
  This minimizes accounting work and your exposure to forgery and theft.

- **Require two signatures on all checks.**
  This eliminates the possibility that one person can access your funds. You may also want to require a third signature for checks exceeding a preset limit for additional protection.

- **Have three people who are authorized to sign checks.**
  This eliminates delaying the processing of a check when a signer is unavailable to countersign a check. It also eliminates the excuse of one person signing a check and processing it because the other signer is unavailable.

- **DO NOT, I repeat, DO NOT sign a blank check.**
  The date, amount and payee's name should be on the check before it is signed to prevent unauthorized persons from cashing it.

- Insist that everyone who receives funds on behalf of the organization, transfer them to the office or treasurer daily if possible.

- **Deposit all cash receipts daily.**
  This maximizes the amount of interest you can earn on these funds and minimizes the opportunity that cash or checks may be lost before they are deposited. It also makes your cash flow and accounts payable management more accurate.
  Another thing to consider is your public image. If someone donates money to you and their check does not clear the bank for two months, they will wonder if you really needed the money or if you are organized well enough to efficiently use the money you have been given.

- **Reconcile your bank statements monthly.**
  If there is a discrepancy, investigate and resolve it immediately.

FUNDRAISING

Unlike governments, you can not print money. If dues from your members are insufficient to meet the budget for your activities, you will have to cut expenses or conduct fundraising activities to earn those additional funds.

These activities will require energies that could be used to benefit your chosen beneficiaries. This means, like other activities, the better you plan and implement the activity, the more successful you will be, and you will receive the largest benefit for the least amount of expended energy.

We will examine some general guidelines, types of activities and planning considerations for fundraising activities.

General Guidelines

First, **do not rush into any new fundraising activity!** This is like investing in a venture that you have not researched. Have your finance committee thoroughly research the activity and submit it to your board for consideration if it appears worthy.

Second, **control expenses!** A lot of activities generate tremendous amounts of revenue only to lose money. Emphasize to your members that your goal is to raise a specified amount of net profit, not revenue. I was involved in a golf tournament where the first year $ 22,000 was lost and the second year a $ 20,000 profit was made and the gross revenues each year were almost identical. The difference was controlling the expenses.

There are several ways to control expenses:

- Obtain materials on consignment. This will eliminate you paying for unused merchandise that you have to inventory after the activity. This merchandise often mysteriously becomes lost and with it the opportunity to pay for itself.
- Minimize your risk by conducting activities with little or no up-front capital requirements.
- If you use an outside fundraiser, negotiate a guarantee, which will protect you if sales do not reach forecasted levels. Also, negotiate who will be responsible for all expenses.

- Confirm the number of meals you will require as late as possible. In addition to maximizing the number of meals you sell in advance, this will minimize the number of unsold meals you purchase. It is unfortunate that many fine activities lose money because too many meals were ordered.
- Delay procuring some items until the last minute. This allows you to reduce quantities or eliminate the items to reduce costs.
- Look to cut expenses up to the date of the activity. By monitoring expected revenue daily up to the event, you will be able to better calculate your expected revenue and make the best possible expense calculation. This effort may make the difference between a profit and a loss.
- Control the amount of freebies that volunteer workers are given or take while participating in the activity. If a volunteer drinks two drinks for every drink he sells, he will cost you more money than he is worth.

Third, **collect revenue from the activity as soon as possible.** An example is selling advance tickets for a meal or an activity. This will commit the people who pay to attend and will help you to gauge your total revenues and expenses, which will help you control expenses and earn the best possible profit. If you do not ask people to pay in advance, they will decide the day of the activity if they will attend. This leaves you vulnerable to weather, other activities that you are competing against and personal/or family reasons for the person not to attend the activity.

Fourth, **deposit receipts from an activity daily.** Holding cash receipts will cost you interest and make your cash flow analysis inaccurate. It will also make you look unprofessional to someone who gave you a check if you haven't cashed it for a few months.

Fifth, **minimize the number of people who handle cash.** If you are conducting a festival, have booths that sell tickets to handle all cash and have the refreshment or souvenir booths take tickets. This will decrease the number of people who are in contact with cash, increase security and make it easier for the workers in the booth because it is easier to take tickets than make change in the booth. It will also be easier to control money for change, periodically monitor revenues during the activity and make management decisions based on more accurate revenue information.

Sixth, **conducting a cash solicitation is like selling, you must ask for the money.** Ask the committee to make the first donations. This reconfirms their commitment to the activity and eliminates a problem when they are asked by a potential donor, "How much did you contribute?" Have your volunteers ask for a specific or recommended amount. People will respond more favorably if they are asked for $ 20 than if you ask them for whatever they want to give. Give each volunteer one prospect who is a sure thing to make a donation. This will build his confidence that the cause is worthy and that he can be successful asking others for money. Once he learns that it is not difficult you have won the battle.

Seventh, **when you need goods or services, ask for a donation.** People too often pay retail for goods or services when they could obtain a donation, if they just asked for it. A lot of businesses because of their cash flow or accounting situation would be happy to donate goods or services when they can not make a cash donation. Create a shopping list for the activity and have your volunteers take it to businesses and ask them for help.

If you can not get an item donated, ask to buy it at cost. If you can not buy it at cost, ask to buy it wholesale. If you can not buy it at wholesale, buy it retail (the last resort) and ask for favorable terms.

Eighth, **maintain good records of your fundraising activities.** These records will tell you who has contributed previously so he can be solicited again. A prior donor is much more likely to donate again (if he feels good about a previous involvement in the activity and with your organization) than a business that has never made a donation. These records can also assist in planning the activity next time or in the event any legal questions arise.

Ninth, **be careful when dealing with celebrities.** This area can be a double edged sword. A celebrity can serve as an honorary chairman to recruit opinion leaders into the activity, write letters, make appearances, etc. and make a positive impact. Then again, some celebrities will be an administrative and financial nightmare. They can demand special flights, hotel suites, limousines, special meals and even massages, which can cost you much more money than the advantage of their appearance raised for your beneficiary.

Tenth, **use written contracts to protect yourself.** Any time you are dealing with money and multiple parties, a contract is essential to prevent misunderstandings and unnecessary financial liability.

A contact needs to include:

- The legal name of all parties.
- The length of time it is in effect.
- Detail the obligations of all parties.
- Specify when it will be terminated and how it can be broken.
- List the methods of recourse for all parties.
- If you operate in multiple states, specify where it is enforceable.
- Discuss consignment of the contract.
- List all warranties.
- List exclusions, such as acts of God.

A contract is of mutual interest and benefit to all parties. Although, gentleman's agreements can be acceptable if you know whom you are dealing with, be suspicious if someone is hesitant to enter into a written contract.

Eleventh, **be careful when you contract with an outside solicitor.** Remember, it is your reputation that is in jeopardy. Thoroughly examine his record before entering into an agreement. Ask him to supply you with the names of organizations similar to your's as references. Call those organizations and any others that you learn used the firm to determine its credibility. Call your local Better Business Bureau and ask if they have received any negative reports on the company. Have your legal counsel review and approve any contract before it is signed. If the solicitor offers you a guarantee, make sure it is in writing and try to get them to put all or part of it into an escrow account. Verify all solicitation laws in your city, county and state, and comply with them to obtain all necessary permits before you sign the contract.

Finally, **selling activity tickets require special guidelines.**

- Number tickets to provide accounting control. Deliver tickets to volunteers in assigned numerical blocks and make sure they know that they will be accountable for returning the tickets and or the money for the tickets.
- Hold regular committee meetings so each volunteer can report his progress, turn money in and obtain more tickets.

- Pre-activity ticket sales are important and can be accelerated by offering discounts or bonuses.
- Divide your volunteers into teams and offer rewards for the teams and individuals that sell the most tickets.
- Make sure that the job of selling tickets is FUN!

Types of Activities

There are several categories of fundraising activities for you to consider. They include:

- **Merchandise sales**—This can include magazines, t-shirts, hats, etc.
- **Food Sales**—Fruit, candy, cakes, etc.
- **Prepared Meals**—Breakfasts, lunches and dinners are all good and can include everything from a pancake breakfast to a fish fry.
- **Event Sales**—This includes garage sales, flea markets, bazaars, auctions, arts and crafts shows, book fairs, etc.
- **Property and Equipment Rentals**—You may rent out a portion of your office facility, parking spaces, or computer time. Special equipment might include casino tables for groups to conduct a Las Vegas night party.
- **Gambling**—Consult with your legal counsel before you conduct an activity in this area. Conduct a Las Vegas night where a business hires you to run a casino. People play with **play money** and can buy a donated prize at the end of the evening with their winnings. The organization makes money by selling refreshments and giving patrons a small amount of play money for a fixed donation.
  Raffling cars, houses, guns and other merchandise can also be very profitable. There is some risk involved so be sure to comply with all legal regulations before beginning the activity.
- **Socials**—These activities are not only fun, but you can make money conducting parties and picnics. A celebrity roast is another social fundraiser where you recruit a celebrity who will allow himself to be roasted. Recruit six to ten roasters and a well known emcee to induce the public to buy tickets for the benefit of the organization and to see one or more of the celebrities.

- **Entertainment**—This area can be very risky if you have a large amount of up-front expenses. It includes concerts, seminars and lectures by celebrity speakers.
- **Sports**—Local bowling, golf, softball, etc. tournaments can be profitable. In addition, sponsoring an event like the Harlem Globetrotters can be rewarding.
- **Services**—This includes car washes, painting addresses on curbs and operating a delivery service.
- **Life Insurance**—The donor buys a life insurance policy and names the organization as the beneficiary. The premiums are tax deductible and the death benefit will substantially help the organization.

As you can see, there are almost an infinite number of types and variations of fundraisers. They can all be successful depending on how well you plan and manage them.

Planning Considerations

Planning a fundraising activity requires all of the planning steps previously discussed in the planning area. In addition, consider several factors when deciding on what type of fundraiser you will conduct and when you will conduct it.

- **Choose the date for the activity.** Consider the season and how the typical weather that time of year will affect the event. A charity golf tournament in Minnesota in March or April might risk failure because of inclement weather.
- **Research the other activities that you will compete against.** If there are established activities in the community that are institutions on certain dates, consider moving your date. An example would be trying to conduct an activity on a fall Saturday in Tuscaloosa, Alabama when the University of Alabama is playing a home football game. You will have a difficult time attracting a lot of people who might normally attend the event.
- **Consider which day of the week to conduct the activity.** Some events will be more successful on one day than on another. An example might be an event at a nightclub. Sundays and Mondays are usually slower nights than Thursday, Friday or Saturday.

- **Try to avoid conducting events on holidays.**
  You will not only have a hard time attracting the paying public, but will also find it difficult to recruit enough volunteers.
- **Remember that people have more money after they are paid.**
  In your area this may mean Friday or the 15th and 30th of the month. This can also be helpful in planning your advance ticket sales strategy and choosing a date for the activity.
- **There is normally less competition during the summer because of vacations, the winter because of weather and the holiday season and on weeknights because of school and work the next day.**

MEMBERSHIP DUES

Most organizations rely on membership dues to raise some or all of the money necessary to conduct their activities.

When you begin to design dues for the organization, consider the types of memberships you wish to offer, dues amounts for each type, billing procedures, payment methods and collection techniques. This preparation will make you more competitive with other organizations and more likely to attract people to join your organization.

Types of Memberships

Before you can determine how much the dues for a member are, you must first decide on the types of memberships you will offer.

There are several types of membership you may wish to offer including:

- **Regular**—This is the type of member that you wish to comprise the majority of the organization in size and participation.
- **Associate**—You may offer these members a slight discount because for one reason or another they can not or do not wish to be regular members.
- **Spouse**—This category allows a husband or a wife to participate equally, but is less expensive than two regular memberships. This allows you to reduce your mailing costs as you would only mail one piece per household.
- **Junior**—You may wish to permit the children of your members to participate in your activities. This will help you to prepare them for becoming regular members when they become of age.
- **Life**—This membership is normally given to a member who has made major contributions to the organization. Three examples are a member who recruits 50 new members in one year, all past presidents and other members the organization deems worthy. I suggest that it be given rarely, which will make it much more coveted by your members.
- **Corporate Sponsorships**—Will encourage businesses to sponsor members. This will be discussed in more detail in the next section.

Dues Amounts

Now that you have established the types of memberships to offer, it is time to determine the amount of dues for each category.

First, establish the length of time that a membership encompasses. A year is common, but some organizations choose longer or shorter periods. Remember that the more often you have to collect a members dues, the more effort will be required in dues collection and the member will have more opportunities not to renew his membership.

Second, if you are affiliated with a state, national or international organization, determine if you will pass through those dues costs in total or whether you will supplement a portion of those dues with your fundraising activities.

Third, based on your budget requirements and size of your organization, determine how much of your budget will be funded by membership dues. For example, if you have a budget of $ 10,000 per year and 100 members, you may not be able to get 100 people to pay $ 100 for membership dues, which will force you to supplement dues income with fundraising activities. Decide on a dollar figure that you would like dues income to provide in your budget.

Finally, review what all competitive groups in your area charge for memberships. Like it or not, you are competing with other groups for your members' time and money. If you raise the dues too high, they will associate with other organizations instead of your organization.

After you have considered all of these factors, forecast your membership size and establish an amount for dues in each category.

Dues Billing Procedures

Sixty days prior to a person's membership expiring, send him a bill with a letter from the president thanking him for his contributions to the organization and encouraging him to renew his membership. As we discussed in the personnel management section, coordinate this with a call from your membership committee. A personal call is more effective than a letter in persuading members who are uncertain about renewing their membership.

Send a second bill thirty days before his membership expires to the members who did not pay his dues after receiving the first bill. A second call from a different person is advisable at this time, and a close personal friend of the member or the president is more likely to be successful.

After his membership expires do not give up! Call him one more time. He should realize by now how important he is to the organization and renew, but if he does not, be gracious and try to learn why he is leaving the organization so you can make any necessary changes to avoid losing any more members.

Methods of Payment

Offer several methods of dues payment as a convenience feature for your members. It alone will help you to recruit and retain more members.

Methods you may offer for the payment of dues include: cash, check, one or more credit cards, payroll deduction, time payment and matching funds from their employer.

Determine ahead of time your policy for insufficient checks because you will receive them for membership dues as well as in your other activities.

Using credit cards like Visa and MasterCard will make dues payment more convenient for your members and can also be used in conjunction with your activities. Contact your bank to establish an account for the credit card and obtain the necessary supplies.

Payroll deduction will not work for everyone, but you should explore the possibility in your environment.

Matching funds are generally only available for organizations that are 501c3 charitable groups. If you qualify, this is an excellent tool to increase your revenue and the impact you can make in your community.

Dues Collection

Collecting the entire dues amount upon billing is preferred to a time payment plan, but you may have little choice. Offer the time payment plan as infrequently as possible and on a case by case basis.

Having an accounts receivable balance creates more work for your staff and treasurer, makes your cash flow planning less accurate, can result in the organization going into debt if they are not managed efficiently and the resulting attitude problems can affect the delinquent and other members. An organization that requires a newly elected board member to sign a bank note to finance a debt is unlikely to attract many good candidates for those board positions.

Once you have established a well planned and designed system of memberships and dues, review each of these areas annually to guarantee you remain effective.

CORPORATE SPONSOR PROGRAM

Fundraising programs that target businesses throughout the year can create several problems. They are:

- Multiple solicitations of the business during the year. Businesses do not like to be continually solicited for contributions. Especially, if they contributed recently.
- Businesses may not be familiar with your organization, which puts you at an immediate disadvantage.
- You will be competing with several other organizations for limited funds from businesses.
- Soliciting funds more than once from a business during a year, leads to wasted volunteer efforts.

A corporate sponsor program can solve these problems. It offers the following benefits to your organization:

- Businesses will make a one time contribution for a 12 month period.
- Businesses will be more familiar with your organization because you will sell them the overall organization instead of sponsoring one activity.
- Your organization will be more competitive with other organizations because you make a united and more professional presentation of your group's activities.
- You will minimize efforts.
- The organization will receive multiple benefits. In addition to the contribution, you may receive members from the business and additional help on other activities that the business was not familiar with previously.

There are several benefits that a business will receive from a corporate sponsorship. Following are some examples of programs you may want to include:

- **Memberships**—They can have a specified number of their employees become members of your organization.
- **Publicity**—Listing in all organization publications.
- **Sponsorship of an activity**—The business will be able to have a banner, publicity and credit for a community oriented activity.

- **Recognition at a sponsor luncheon**—A nice benefit is to have a luncheon annually where you recognize and thank all of your corporate sponsors. This tells them how important they are to your organization, shows them that other businesses also find your community work important and sets the stage for asking them to renew their sponsorship next year.

Prestige and ego also are an important consideration when designing your program. Establish several different levels of sponsorship. Have a level for the smallest business and one for the largest. Use names such as diamond, gold, silver, etc. to make the sponsorships sound prestigious. Vary the price for each level and the benefits based on your local environment. An example might be that a gold sponsorship would offer 10 memberships, a sponsorship of 2 activities, the business listed in all publications and recognition at the sponsorship luncheon.

Take very good care of the businesses that become sponsors. Like members they are the easiest to resell next year, but they will not renew their sponsorship if you do not deliver what you promised.

Establish one board member who will be solely responsible for selling corporate sponsorships. Create a brochure that will describe the organization and a slide show that can be used in presentations. He must keep a good record of the businesses that are contacted and their responses. If this is not done, time may be wasted in the future calling on businesses that are not interested and opportunities may be lost by not calling back businesses that were interested, but could not buy a sponsorship at the moment when they were contacted.

MISCELLANEOUS MEMBER SERVICES

In addition to membership dues and fundraising activities, you may wish to offer one or more programs to raise money for the organization and benefit your individual members.

With board approval, contract to offer one or more of the following programs at a discount to your members, with the organization receiving a percentage of the volume of business that is generated by the organization's members.

- **Insurance**—This might include life, automobile, health or any other insurance program you feel will benefit your members.
- **Discount Tickets**—This can include tickets for movies, airlines, amusement parks, sports events, etc.
- **Coupons**—Similar to discount tickets, but it may provide you additional opportunities for discount products such as hotel rooms or meals.
- **Credit Cards**—You may be able to qualify as a sponsor for a bank-type credit card, which would give the member a competitive interest rate and the organization a percentage of all business transacted with the cards.
- **Credit Union** -Although this requires regulatory approval and capital, you may want to establish a credit union to meet the financial savings and borrowing needs of your members.
- **Store**—Depending on your physical layout and demand, a product store offers the members the opportunity to buy organization related supplies or other beneficial products conveniently and at a competitive price. If you are a part of a state, national or international organization, you may want to stock products they offer and supplement them with additional products.

These types of services can be beneficial, but do a complete risk vs. benefit analysis before you commit your organization to a financial risk.

ORGANIZATION TREASURER

The treasurer is the chief financial officer of the organization. It is advantageous for you to have a certified public accountant as your treasurer. They have the knowledge and experience to manage your organization's financial needs.

Using the by-laws and budget, the treasurer is the "Dr. No" of the organization. It is his job to exercise fiduciary responsibility over the assets of the organization. That usually means saying "No" to people who would like to flex the rules. If a treasurer does not adhere to the rules, the organization will usually suffer.

The treasurer is responsible for all matters relating to the financial welfare of the organization. He is responsible to:

- **Control all bank accounts.** Establish as few bank accounts as possible. Require two signatures on all checks including the treasurer's. One of the other two signers should be the president. Have all bank statements mailed to one location and to the attention of the treasurer. This responsibility includes approving that all expenditures are in your budget, paying all bills and making sure all monies are deposited into the bank the same day they are received. Do not allow the person who writes the checks to handle the money and make the deposits. This provides you with a check and balance and will offer additional protection to your assets.

- **Collect all funds due to the organization.** This will include delinquent dues and payments for organization activities.

- **File all reports required by all governmental agencies.** The most common reports are your annual tax return, quarterly 990 forms and social security withholding for your paid staff.

- **Serve as a member of the finance committee.** This committee reviews and recommends new ways and means activities to the board for approval, researches and recommends to the board investments for the organization's assets and regularly discusses items that affect the financial status of the organization.

- **Regularly report to the board of directors the financial status of the organization.** Write these reports in addition to making a verbal report. Have the written reports show a cash flow analysis, budget month to date and year to date and the status and previous month's activity of all bank accounts and investments.

- **Present the board a summary each quarter.** This is critical for the board to conduct its quarterly review and revision of the annual plan.
- **Complete an annual audit and submit an annual financial statement to the board of directors.**

You may wish to add board and non-board members to assist the treasurer in performing these duties. Assign them to report to the treasurer and normally they would not have signatory authority over any of the assets of the organization.

INTERNAL
COMMUNICATIONS

"Never tell people how to do things. Tell them what to do and they will surprise you with their ingenuity."

George S. Patton, Jr.

INTERNAL COMMUNICATIONS

Maintaining effective internal communications is imperative in order to insure that your organization is successful. Internal communications aim to make the members proud of belonging to the organization, inform them of what the organization is involved with and motivate them to participate in achieving the goals of the organization.

Your meetings are the best place to communicate to your members the business of the organization. (Refer to the personnel management section for the discussion on conducting effective meetings.)

ORGANIZATION SECRETARY

The secretary of a voluntary organization is responsible for all communications. The secretary should be a member of the executive committee.

The secretary's responsibilities include:

1. Agenda and minutes for all membership and board meetings.
2. Publications
3. Organization History
4. Rosters
5. Annual Calendar

Agendas And Minutes

The secretary prepares all membership and board meeting agendas with the approval of the president.

If possible, mailing the agenda with the previous meeting's minutes will remind people of the upcoming meeting, let them know what will be discussed and what was discussed at the last meeting.

If you have a computer, it is an excellent way to take the minutes of a meeting. When the meeting is over all you have to do is print the minutes and they're ready to distribute and file.

If you take minutes by hand or on the computer, it is advisable to tape the meeting to make sure all crucial details are recorded in the minutes.

PUBLICATIONS

There are two questions to address when you design publications for your organization. They are:

1. **Who is your audience?** Part of your member survey should determine the demographics of your audience and what they want in a publication.
2. **What is your budget?**
   A. How much does it cost to produce your selected format? For a newsletter this would include paper and artwork.
   B. What are the mailing costs, if applicable? Check with the post office concerning a bulk rate mailing permit. This can not only reduce your mailing costs, but may influence the physical size of the publication to meet postal regulations.
   C. What is the frequency that you will publish and distribute the publication? Monthly, bi-monthly, etc.

Once we have answered these questions, we can now examine five different publications.

1. **NEWSLETTERS**

   The two most important qualities of an effective newsletter are that it is **ON TIME AND ACCURATE** . If the newsletter is published monthly and arrives two weeks late or does not have accurate details of your activities, your membership will stop reading it because they will feel that it is not worth their valuable time.

   What are the benefits of a newsletter?

   - It communicates the current activities of the organization.
   - The calendar gives the audience the ability to plan their schedule.
   - Builds pride in the organization.
   - Creates enthusiasm for your activities.
   - Recognizes people for their contributions.
   - Provides a historical record of the organization's activities.

   Your newsletter can contain several types of information.

   - **Calendar of Events**—Allows members to plan their schedule. A reference note to the page of an article about the activity makes it easier for your readers to find the details about the activity. Listing a six week calendar (or longer) in a monthly newsletter provides your members the opportunity to plan their personal calendars further in advance, which will increase participation in your activities.

- **Upcoming Activities**—These stories should be written by the activity chairman if possible. Be sure to acknowledge sub-chairmen and/or other volunteers involved in the activity. Put all names in BOLD type. Everyone likes to read his name in print. This will help you to recruit more volunteers because your members will feel that their efforts are appreciated.

- **Completed Activities**—These stories contain details about completed activities. Again, thank your volunteers by listing their names. Also list any businesses that contributed to the activity and mail them a copy of the newsletter with or after your thank you letter.

- **Awards Received**—List awards received by the organization or the members. Again you have the opportunity to say thank you for their contributions. These successes will build pride in the organization and motivate others to volunteer for activities.

- **Upcoming programs and or speakers**—Enthusiasm should be used in promoting upcoming meetings and your program or speaker to encourage your members to attend the meeting.

- **New Members**—This welcomes the new member into the organization. Seeing their name in the newsletter reinforces their decision to join the organization. This is also a good reference list for recruiting activity chairmen, sub-chairmen and volunteers.

- **Members due to renew their membership**—This is one more reminder in addition to mailing a dues notice. Because of a recent change of address, you may renew a member who did not receive their dues notice. Seeing his name in the newsletter reminds him to pay his dues and reinforces his involvement in the organization.

- **Birthdays**—Another reason to list the names of your members.
- **Special announcements**—These can include weddings and the birth of children.
- **President's Comments**—The opportunity for the president to thank, motivate, excite and inspire the members to increased levels of participation.
- **Sponsor recognition**—This section recognizes all corporate sponsors and their contributions.
- **Call to action**—A list of actions that the president and or board recommend to the membership. This may include writing a letter to a legislator or business.
- **Advertisements**—A decision must be made whether or not you will have advertisements in the newsletter. If you have advertising, should it be restricted to members only? Advertising offers you the opportunity to offset or defray the expenses of producing the newsletter.
- **Information from a state or national office**—If applicable, this can be a helpful supplement to your newsletter.
- **Photographs**—The only thing better than a member seeing his name in a newsletter is seeing his picture. This will also help in recruiting more volunteers for activities.

2. NEWSTAPES

A relatively new idea is to publish a newsletter on a cassette tape instead of a paper format. This technology may be received better by your membership and less expensive to produce. Collect articles or information as you would in preparing a newsletter. Instead of printing the information, record it on audio cassettes. Distribute the cassettes by mail. If your newsletter is not producing the results you desire, you may want to investigate this alternative.

3. SPECIAL MAILOUTS

These may be in the form of a post card or letter. Their purpose is to reinforce the importance of a meeting or activity and to communicate activities that came up after the newsletter was published.

4. **BROCHURE**

   An organizational brochure can be used for membership or corporate sponsorship recruiting. It can also be included in the new member kit and for publicity purposes.

5. **ANNUAL REPORT**

   Producing an annual report can offer you the following benefits:

   - **Historical**—Gives an annual performance evaluation of the organization for future reference.
   - **Publicity**—To enhance the image of the organization in the community.
   - **Sponsorships**—The annual report is an excellent tool to show prospective corporate sponsors the impact your organization makes on your community.

OTHER COMMUNICATION TOOLS

In addition to the publications discussed above, the following tools can also be utilized in communicating to your membership.

- **Answering Machine**—If you have an office or not, you can use an answering machine two ways.
  - On your regular phone line the machine can be used to provide announcements and take messages.
  - On a special phone line the machine can be used as a 24 hour a day message center. This is where any member can phone and hear of all upcoming meetings and activities. Regular updating is critical. Like a newsletter, if the information is not timely or accurate, your members will stop using the system. Humor or incentives can be used to motivate members to use the system.

- **Automated Calling Unit**—These units are designed and primarily used for telephone sales. They can save you time notifying your membership about activities by being an answering machine in reverse that calls your entire membership.

- **Computer**—In addition to providing administrative assistance, a computer will allow you to set up a bulletin board where members call the computer via a modem from their computer. Activity information is stored on the computer for retrieval by the member.

- **Phone Banks**—A committee that will divide and telephone the membership about an activity.

- **Television and radio**—With the advent of cable television, activities can be published for the public as well as the membership. Local community access channels are available for written announcements and airing programs that you produce about your organization. Airing your own program on a local radio station is another excellent communications tool.

ORGANIZATION HISTORY

Establishing and maintaining a history of the organization is important. It can serve the current membership by revealing established precedents and documenting accomplishments which increase credibility and build pride in the membership.

New organizations have a unique opportunity to save first person accounts of their activities from the date their group is conceived. It is easy to think that this information is not important, but it is. Take the time to document your activities!

Three types of history can be assembled:

- **Written**—This includes meeting and board meeting agendas and minutes, newsletters, annual reports, correspondence, financial records, membership records, annual plans and activity plans.
- **Audio/Video**—Audio and video records can be of activities, meetings, etc. Another use of audio and video records is to tape past members and presidents talking about their participation in the organization. This offers not only the details of what happened, but a personal insight that is missing in a written record.

Create an elected or appointed position to the board of directors for a historian. This will not only dedicate at least one person in the organization to work on your history, but it will also give that position recognition and respect. By placing this emphasis on the history of your organization, you will communicate its importance to your membership.

MEMBERSHIP ROSTERS

Producing a roster of your membership is helpful in encouraging communications between members.

- **Types of rosters**
  Several types of rosters can be produced and each has its own purpose.
  — Alphabetic
  — Membership Renewal Date—This can be used by your retention and activation committees.
  — By Zip Code in mailing label format—Photocopying this roster on pressure sensitive labels will allow you to save time in addressing newsletters and other publications.
  — Board of Directors
  — Past Members

- **How often should you publish your rosters?**
  You must decide how often each roster should be produced. This can vary based on how fast your membership grows, how often people move, board changes, etc.

- **The use and restriction of use of your membership roster.**
  This is an important decision for your board of directors.
  We recommend that you beware of giving your roster to non-members or letting your members use rosters for solicitations. Most people do not want to have their name given out for use by a solicitor.

CALENDARS

As discussed in the planning area, establishing an annual calendar is a natural extension of planning your goals and activities.

Once the annual calendar has been planned, it can be distributed to the membership, print the appropriate portion of it in the newsletter and or be used for modifying or adding activities to it during the year.

ONE-ON ONE-COMMUNICATIONS

One-on-one communications with your board and membership falls into three types.

- **Written**—This is often the least used, but most effective. You can use several types of written notes and letters to enhance your image as an effective leader.
  - — Thank you notes—These personal handwritten notes are the most effective and least utilized of all written letters. This shows that you care and appreciated the person enough to take time out of your busy schedule to write.
  - — Follow-Up letter—This is the second least used letter and gives a progress report.
  - — Confirmation letter—Confirms details discussed about a topic.
  - — Instruction letter—Insures that the recipient knows what you expect them to do.
  - — Letter of appreciation—This letter recognizes someone for his contribution. It is formal and similar to a thank you note.

- **Telephone**—To save time when using the telephone, have an agenda of what you would like to discuss before you make the call. The last item on the agenda is to set a follow-up call or meeting.

- **In Person**—This is the best verbal way to communicate because each of you can see the reaction of the other person to the business discussed. Like telephone communications, use an agenda and a follow-up date should be the last item discussed.

Lunch meetings have been popular for many years. Breakfast meetings have gained in popularity in recent years as people try to find ways to accomplish more in less time.

PUBLIC RELATIONS

"A lot of people don't have much to say, and that's fine. The trouble with some of them is you have to listen a long time to find it out."

Author Unknown

PUBLIC RELATIONS

The public relations area is responsible for communicating information and a desired image to the community.

Making the organization appear professional, planning an annual public relations plan, publicizing activities and effectively working with media representatives are imperative in order to achieve the image in the community that you desire.

MAKING YOUR ORGANIZATION APPEAR PROFESSIONAL

Appearing professional in the community will enhance your image and make people more receptive to your programs and ideas. This must be accomplished before media representatives will take your organization seriously.

Often overlooked, but very important tools that will enhance your professional image are letterhead, envelopes, business cards and invoices.

- **Letterhead**—Print your logo on your stationery. If you do not have a logo, design one that represents your organization. Printing your board members names and the companies they represent on the stationery is good publicity for them and their companies.
- **Envelopes**—Include your logo on your envelopes. The added expense is small compared to the benefits it offers.
- **Business Cards**—Supply cards for your President and Executive Director (if you have one). Provide cards to other board members as desirable.
- **Invoices**—Formal invoices are used for dues billing and other services rendered (i.e. fundraising) and are more effective than typing an invoice on your letterhead.

ANNUAL PUBLIC RELATIONS PLAN

As a by-product of completing the organization's annual plan, an annual public relations plan should be completed.

After the activity calendar has been planned, prioritize activities by importance for attempting to obtain publicity.

- Plan the right type of publicity for each event. Appearing on a television talk show may not be practical for every event. Some events may justify only newspaper coverage while some may justify newspaper, radio and television.
- Do not attempt to obtain publicity on every event if you are a very active organization. If you submit press releases and request radio and television coverage every week, the media will become callous toward the organization.
- Balance your calendar so you do not schedule all of your major activities in a short time frame. These are the events that you will want to receive the most publicity and if they are spread out during the year you will receive more coverage.

Have one person responsible for all publicity. Everyone in the organization should coordinate their publicity needs with this person. One person can build a rapport with the media contacts, while several people contacting the media will be detrimental to your efforts. Controlling your people will earn you respect with the media and they will be more receptive when they are approached by your organization.

Design a fill in the blank press release form for the organization. This will make the public relations director's job easier because it will make all releases uniform and allow the activity sub-chairman to prepare them for release. Have a check off box for indicating the type of media coverage requested (television, radio, newspaper, etc.), contact name, phone number and the details of the activity to be publicized. Once the form has been reviewed and approved by the public relations director, it can be typed and distributed.

The public relations director should contact media sources upon taking office. Asking them for suggestions on how to work with them will communicate your interest in making their job easier plus you will learn information that will make your job easier as well. This is also an excellent time to distribute your annual media guide, which I will discuss in more detail in this section.

MEDIA DIRECTORY

The public relations director compiles a complete list of all media sources and contacts in your area. If this has already been done, revise at least annually.

The more information the directory contains, the more of your members' time it will save and the more professional your organization will appear to the media.

Include the following information in your directory:

- Name of the station, newspaper, etc.
- Contact Names—General Manager, assignments editor, news director and appropriate personalities.
- Address—Include the post office box for mailing purposes and the street address for directional purposes.
- Phone Number and extension of all contacts.
- List of special programs such as talk shows and community affairs programs. Include the day that they air, the time and the deadline for booking an appearance.
- Public service announcement (PSA) policies.
- Photo Policies—Do they prefer black and white to color photos? Are slides acceptable or negatives preferred? What kind of description do they desire?
- List the types of events that they like to cover and the events that they request that you submit the information.
- Days of the week that you are more likely to receive coverage.

MEDIA GUIDE

The media guide is designed to quickly inform the media about the purpose and activities of your organization. Revise it annually and hand deliver it to all appropriate media contacts. Be aware of new media personalities, reporters and managers who move into town or into a new responsibility. Congratulate them on their new opportunity and use your visit to introduce your organization and distribute a media guide to them. The president, public relations director and any other appropriate officers should carry them at all times. It is surprising how may opportunities arise for you to distribute them at a meeting or an activity.

Components of an effective media guide include:

- **Folder or Cover Letter**—Your organization's name should be prominently displayed.
- **Organization Fact Sheet**—Include your purpose, number of members, significant historical facts, past accomplishments, awards received, dates of your meetings and the name and phone number of your public relations director and president. This fact sheet can also be used in a corporate recruitment package.
- **Annual calendar of activities.**
- **Highlight activities**—Include newsworthy and human interest activities. This will create interest in an upcoming activity.
- **All current news releases**—This may stimulate immediate coverage of your activities.
- **A biography of your new president**—Include his employer, other organizations that he is involved in, family information, hometown and awards received. This not only adds prestige to the office of president, but will make his employer, family, hometown and other organizations proud of him and your organization. They will be more likely to support your organization.
- **List your board of directors and their employers.**
- **List the name and phone number of the public relations director and the president so the media can contact them for additional information or for interviews.**

PUBLICIZING AN ACTIVITY

To effectively convince the media to publicize an activity, you must think like them. They look for stories that are newsworthy or have a human interest appeal.

After the activity plan is written, decide on the type and number of press releases that you will distribute. Pre-write all the releases for the entire duration of the activity at that time. Leave blanks to add names, numbers and details as the activity progresses. Pre-plan the dates for distribution of the releases. Consider the day of the week or other special event competition when planning your distribution dates. Even with this planning, if a major story breaks on your distribution date, the amount of coverage you will receive will decline.

Types of activity press releases are: announcing the beginning of the activity, updating progress to date, the day of the activity announcement and a post activity release to announce the results of the activity and thank the people who participated.

Rules for press releases vary for the written and electronic (television and radio) media and we will examine them individually.

Written Press Releases

- Typewritten
- Double Spaced
- One page maximum
- One side of the page
- Include the organization's contact name and phone number at the top. List the work and home number.
- Emphasize the date that the information can be publicized at the top. This will prevent any stories being published too soon.
- Have the most important information in the first paragraph.
- Remember to include:
  - WHO—is conducting the activity and whom it benefits.
  - WHY—it is being conducted.
  - WHAT—the activity is and the most important details.
  - WHERE—the activity will take place. Make sure to list the name of the location and appropriate directions.
  - WHEN—This includes the day of the week, month, date, year, time and a.m. or p.m.

- Photos—Check with the media representative to see if they prefer black and white or color photos. Make sure to include a description of the photo.

So often a group distributes a release for a great activity, but they forget one of these details. Doing so discounts the credibility of the release because people will question the accuracy of the other information. Also, people will not normally go out of their way to find out these details.

SAMPLE

CONTACT: BILL FRANK
(0) 123-555-1234
(H) 123-555-4321

FOR IMMEDIATE RELEASE

The XYZ club of Greenville will hold a 2 man scramble golf tournament to benefit Cerebral Palsy on Wednesday, May 15, 1987 at 8:00 a.m. at the Greenville Country Club.

Entry fees are $ 50 per person and include a barbecue lunch, cart, green fees and a post tournament party. The top three teams will receive trophies and a long drive contest will be held.

William Smith of Greenville, all pro with the Strokers baseball team will serve as the celebrity host of the tournament.

For further information contact, Bill Frank at 555-1234 or Joe Jones at 555-9876.

-30-

Radio and Television Publicity

- Contact the media source well in advance of your desired air date. Because you will produce an audio or video tape, time must be allowed for producing the tape.
- Meet with the appropriate contact at the station to plan the desired publicity for the activity.
  - Decide on the type of spot and its length.
  - Targeted air dates.
  - Technical requirements—This includes visual aids, sound system, studio props, on-site location, the need for a voice over, etc.
  - Schedule the production date.
  - Ask the media representative for additional copies to distribute to other stations. This may not be appropriate if the station is co-sponsoring the activity.
- Write the script in the specified format of the station.
- Have the media representative review and revise the script.
- If you are using a "personality," allow them to review and approve the script. Also, verify that the production date is acceptable to them.
- Once the tape is completed and copied, hand deliver the copies to the other stations and save the master.
- Send a thank you letter to the station, media representative and the "personality" for their contribution.
- If appropriate, publicly thank the station with a note in your organization's newsletter and local newspaper. Sometimes, businesses do not want public recognition because it will stimulate others to request donations from them.

Special Ideas

- Recruit media representatives to join your organization. They can contribute to the organization, help you obtain more publicity and help you establish an effective publicity campaign and produce professional press releases.

- Ask newspapers, radio and television stations to co-sponsor an activity. They will receive good publicity and your organization will not only receive more publicity, but will help make the activity more successful.

- Invite media "personalities" to be your guest at activities. If you are conducting a golf tournament, invite the television sports director. This will insure that you will receive the maximum possible publicity.

- Outstanding Citizen Awards—This is a great activity that recognizes outstanding citizens in your community and can be an excellent source for good publicity for your organization.

- Cable Television—Many communities have cable television stations dedicated for community activities. They are good sources for public service announcements. They are also an excellent source for airing your own programs about your organization and activities. Check with the cable company because quite often they will teach you how to produce a program and have the necessary equipment available at no charge for you to borrow.

- Radio Shows—Discuss the possibility of having a radio show for your organization with stations in your area. A five, ten or fifteen minute show once a week can offer many benefits to your organization.

- Newspaper columns—Like the radio show, discuss the advantages of having a regular column in a newspaper, or other publication.

- Community Calendar—Make sure that your organization's meetings and activities are regularly publicized in your newspaper(s), chamber of commerce calendar and all other local or statewide periodicals.

Media Recognition

It is important to recognize the contributions of the media to your organization. Recognition will help you to work more effectively with them in the immediate and long term future.

Be sure to send all media representatives who were involved in an activity a personal thank you note the day of the activity. They will appreciate it very much as they are not thanked enough for their contributions, and very seldom do they receive a formal thank you letter. Letters should be sent to the general manager or editor, and the individual reporters and representatives.

Conduct an annual media reception. The agenda should include the presentation of certificates or plaques to the representatives of the media, presenting the annual report of the organization so they will know what you have accomplished, and distributing the new media guide. You will have the opportunity to meet the representatives in an environment where they are not under pressure to meet a deadline or rush to the next story. Building a personal relationship will be helpful both for them and you when you begin to publicize your next activity.

Recognize a television station, radio station, newspaper, etc. that has co-sponsored an activity with you. Present them a certificate or a plaque at a membership meeting. Make the presentation special so they will know how appreciative you really are. Remember, that the media receives many more requests for publicity and sponsoring events than they could ever possibly accept, and their acceptance of your request shows they care about you and the activity that you are conducting.

CONCLUSION

The media can be a tremendous asset to your organization if you establish a working relationship based on mutual respect. Remember, they are trying to do a job. If you treat them honestly and provide them with the information that they request, you will find them to be a valuable asset. However if you prove unreliable, evasive, refuse to comment, are nervous or become angry they will question the information you have provided to them. If they find that you have been dishonest or insincere in working with them both you and your organization will suffer the consequences.

Although you do not have to be a pro to work with the media, if you use professional techniques, you will find them more receptive to your organization.

APPENDIX

FAVORITE MOTIVATIONAL QUOTATIONS

1. "Destiny is not a matter of chance; it is a matter of choice."
   William Jennings Bryan

2. "One man can make a difference, and every man should try."
   John F. Kennedy

3. "You can because you think you can."
   Roman Poet Virgil

4. "If you want to be successful, you have got to feel the pain."

5. "The secret of success in life is for a person to be ready when his opportunity comes." Disraeli

6. "A man's capacity is usually relative to his goals."

7. "Desire is that ingredient that turns mediocrity into success."

8. "It's amazing what one can accomplish when one doesn't know what one can't do."

9. "To tolerate mediocrity is to foster it." Henry B. Lewis

10. DEDICATION—"The ability and determination to complete a resolution long after the mood in which it was made is gone."

11. "A stranger is just a friend that you have not met yet."

12. "IF NOT YOU WHO, IF NOT NOW WHEN?"
    President Ronald Reagan, 1981 U.S. Jaycee Convention

13. "Success is more a journey than a destination."

14. "Nothing great was ever achieved without enthusiasm." Ralph Emerson

15. "The opposite of winning is not losing, it is quitting."

16. "If you can't do everything, then what is it that you can not fail to do?" Dr. Ray Martens

17. "The mortal enemy of best is good." H. E. Butt

18. "Not doing more than the average is what keeps the average down."

19. "It is better to aim your spirit at the sun and strike an eagle, than to aim it at an eagle and strike a rock."

20. "The dictionary is the only place in the world where success comes before work."

21. "Nothing in this world can take the place of persistence. Talent will not; nothing is more common than unsuccessful men with talent. Genius will not; unrewarded genius is almost a proverb. Education will not; the world is full of educated derelicts. Persistence and determination alone are omnipotent. The slogan "PRESS ON" has solved and always will solve the problems of the human race."
President Calvin Coolidge

22. "Ask not what your country can do for you. Ask what you can do for your country." President John Kennedy (1/20/61)

23. "To be born a free man is an accident. To live as a free man is a responsibility. But, to die a free man is an obligation." John Ben Shepperd, past Texas Attorney General and Secretary of State, and United States Jaycees President

24. "Never Quit, Never Quit, Never Quit, Never Quit; Never, Never, Never, Never Quit!" Winston Churchill

25. "It is the greatest of all mistakes to do nothing because you can do only a little. Do what you can." Sydney Smith

BIBLIOGRAPHY

Warner, Irving; *The Art of Fundraising,* New York, Harper & Row 1975

Sheridan, Philip; *Fundraising for the Small Organization,* New York, M. Evans & Co., 1960

U. S. Jaycees, *Chapter President's Handbook*, Tulsa, 1983

INDEX

ORDER FORM

VOLUNTEER CONCEPTS • P.O. BOX 27584 • AUSTIN, TX 78755

Please send me the following books: QTY.

The Volunteer Handbook   _____ @ $12.95 = _____

Postage & Handling   _____ @ $ 1.50 = _____

Sales Tax @ 8.0% (Texas Residents)   = _____

Total Amount Due   = _____

SHIP TO:

_____

_____   Method of Payment

_____   ____ Check

_____   ____ Money Order

- -

ORDER FORM

VOLUNTEER CONCEPTS • P.O. BOX 27584 • AUSTIN, TX 78755

Please send me the following books: QTY.

The Volunteer Handbook   _____ @ $12.95 = _____

Postage & Handling   _____ @ $ 1.50 = _____

Sales Tax @ 8.0% (Texas Residents)   = _____

Total Amount Due   = _____

SHIP TO:

_____

_____   Method of Payment

_____   ____ Check

_____   ____ Money Order

- -

ORDER FORM

VOLUNTEER CONCEPTS • P.O. BOX 27584 • AUSTIN, TX 78755

Please send me the following books: QTY.

The Volunteer Handbook   _____ @ $12.95 = _____

Postage & Handling   _____ @ $ 1.50 = _____

Sales Tax @ 8.0% (Texas Residents)   = _____

Total Amount Due   = _____

SHIP TO:

_____

_____   Method of Payment

_____   ____ Check

_____   ____ Money Order

- -